THE ROAD TO RECOGNITION

SETH PRICE / BARRY FELDMAN

THE A-TO-Z GUIDE TO PERSONAL BRANDING FOR ACCELERATING YOUR PROFESSIONAL SUCCESS IN THE AGE OF DIGITAL MEDIA

Published in the United States by IdeaPress Publishing.
IDEAPRESS PUBLISHING
www.ideapresspublishing.com

All trademarks are the property of their respective companies.
Cover design: Studio laPlancha

ISBN: 978-1-940858-36-4
ISBN: 978-1-940858-37-1 (e-book)
PROUDLY PRINTED IN THE UNITED STATES OF AMERICA

SPECIAL SALES
IdeaPress Books are available at a special discount for bulk purchases for
sales promotions and premiums, or for use in corporate training programs.
Special editions, including personalized covers, custom forewords,
corporate imprints and bonus content are also available. For more details,
email info@ideapresspublishing.com.

No animals were harmed in the writing, printing or distribution of this book.
The trees, unfortunately, were not so lucky.

THE ROAD TO RECOGNITION

To Jayna and Leah, my teenage daughters, who
are soon to begin rocking down roads of
their own,
Barry

To my aunt Helen who taught me how to thrive in
adversity. And, for my amazing children:
Aidan, Emmanuel, Ava, and Julien,
Seth

Praise for *The Road to Recognition*

"Clever, fun and about as comprehensive a guide as you'll find anywhere."
ANN HANDLEY, author of *Everybody Writes* and *Content Rules*

"Current, useful, actionable and true. It's gold!"
JAY BAER, author of *Youtility* and *Hug Your Haters*

"Deceptively simple, yet incredibly effective. Read it, act on it, and then be patient. You won't be sorry."
JOE PULIZZI, author of *Content Inc.* and *Epic Content*

"If you want to build a personal brand in the digital age, this should be your bible."
BRIAN DEAN, founder of Backlinko.com

"This highly actionable book explains exactly how to create and scale your personal brand."
BRAD INMAN, founder of Inman News

"Personal branding is a necessity in today's marketplace. This quick and easy guide shows you how to do it with heart and verve."
DORIE CLARK, author of *Stand Out* and *Reinventing You*

"This is a clear and concise guide to what might be the most important skill in today's marketplace. Smart, funny, authentic and super-helpful. Do what these guys say and you will reap the rewards."
DOUG KESSLER, co-founder of Velocity Partners

"Building your personal brand is important for anyone who wants to lead a team, build a business, achieve success, and make a difference. Seth and Barry, two leading voices on this important topic, provide actionable advice for building an effective personal brand. If you want to achieve success in your career on your own terms, you need to read this book."
MICHAEL BRENNER, author of *The Content Formula*

"This is the most complete (and engaging) book on the topic of personal branding ever created. Get a copy. Apply the lessons. Enjoy your ascent. Getting recognized for your area of expertise is the name of the game. Bravo Barry and Seth."
ANDY CRESTODINA, author of *Content Chemistry*

"Puts the art of brand building into a measurable, fun, learning experience that will literally put you on the digital map for years to come."
LAURA MONROE, VP of industry and strategic development at RealSatisfied

"Growing professional influence is on the list of every fast-tracking professional in the business world. *The Road to Recognition* does a great job of combining clever design with succinct, actionable tips on everything from authenticity to audience targeting to help you on your path to brandividual success."
LEE ODDEN, author of *Optimize*

"Personal branding is all about building rapport at scale. And rapport is one of the most fundamental sales techniques. Seth and Barry have outlined a simple roadmap for building relationships and recognition in the digital age. This is a must read."
MARK ROBERGE, author of *Sales Acceleration Formula*

"If you're a living, breathing human being doing business in this world, you're a brand, and no one understands that more than Seth and Barry. Here is a roadmap to success worth reading."
NOBU HATA, director of member engagement for the National Association of REALTORS®

"This book is a valuable primer on how to develop a voice that, by benefiting others, will amplify your success."
PAM O'CONNOR, CEO of Leading Real Estate Companies of the World

"Seth and Barry have done a wonderful job of breaking down how to set yourself apart from the rest of the pack with some easy-to-understand concepts that are instantly implementable."
STEPHEN SCHWEICKART, CEO of VScreen & partner at Angel Bespoke

"*The Road to Recognition* is one of those books that reminds me of how I felt while reading Gary Vaynerchuk's first book, *Crush It*. As I read I'm making a list of everyone I want to send this book to."
STEPHANIE CHUMBLEY, director of new media and education at Chicago Title Company of Oregon

"These days, everyone has a brand. Everyone. And that brand matters a lot. This book shows you the how, what, and why of personal branding in the digital age. Well done!"
MARCUS SHERIDAN, author of *They Ask, You Answer*

"Personal branding is a language that's best learned via a guided journey. Read this book to master individual differentiation in the land of information overload we call the web."
FREDERICK TOWNES, co-founder of Placester

"This is simply the speak-n-spell of personal branding! If you're looking for a simple and pragmatic way to build your personal brand, look no further. You absolutely need to work your way through the alphabet of *The Road to Recognition*. Each letter, errr chapter, helps you master a rich language of building a strategy that will take your career to the next level."
ROBERT ROSE, author of *Experiences: The Seventh Era of Marketing*

"A first of its kind—a field manual for personal branding in today's information age. Its value is priceless for those wishing to succeed professionally."
CHAD POLITT, VP of Audience and partner at Native Adversiting Institute

"You have to read this book. While digital marketing is always in a state of flux, the fundamentals never change. Seth Price and Barry Feldman have distilled the art of personal branding into 26 easy-to-understand chapters so that anyone can take immediate action and dramatically increase their brand presence."
SUJAN PATEL, author of *The Content Marketing Playbook*

"*The Road to Recognition* is the only book about building a personal brand that you will ever need to read. Most business books have one kickass takeaway. This one has 26."
CHRIS SMITH, author of *The Conversion Code*

"Having a strong personal brand and communicating it is more important than ever. *The Road to Recognition* will help you map out the journey of personal branding. I love the style—easy to read and entertaining but packed with amazing advice on how to build YOUR brand."
LAURIE WESTON DAVIS, CEO of Better Homes and Gardens Real Estate

"When it comes to building your brand, it's a jungle out there. Between blogging, social media, landing pages and email, there's so much to manage in today's always-on, always-connected universe. Seth Price and Barry Feldman distill years of marketing and technology experience into an elegant blueprint that can be easily put into action by anyone."
STEFAN SWANEPOEL, author of *Surviving Your Serengeti*

"*The Road to Recognition* provides a sensible A-to-Z guide to personal branding that can work for anyone. Once you accept your personal brand is mission-critical in the digital age, you need to read this book."
BERNIE BORGES, CEO of Find and Convert

"If you need to learn about branding—and you do—this is the book."
ALONZO BODDEN, comedian, winner of NBC's Last Comic Standing

"Seth and Barry have simplified the roadmap for building your personal brand in today's marketplace. All you need now is the commitment to do the work required to connect with your audience."
KRISHNA GUPTA, founder & managing partner of Romulus Capital

"There are plenty of smart people and resources in this industry, but few think about the delivery and reader experience like Seth and Barry. If you're a believer in books that are both nutritious AND delicious, you're in luck."
JAY ACUNZO, founder of Unthinkable.fm

"Essential reading for anyone looking to accelerate the process of establishing a recognized personal brand."
JAKE ANDERSON, co-founder of FertilityIQ

"You need a personal brand and Seth and Barry nail it on how to develop one—from A-to-Z. A must read!"
DR. NICK MORGAN, author of *Power Cues* and *Trust Me*

"If you don't tell your story, somebody else will. In *The Road To Recognition*, Seth Price and Barry Feldman give entrepreneurs a fast and dynamic playbook for growing and keeping the friends and fans essential for building your business."
AUDIE CHAMBERLAIN, CEO of Lion & Orb

Foreword

People who like kale rarely overlook opportunities to tell you how much you're missing out if you don't eat kale.

People who like kale swear its importance transcends the banal categorization of "vegetable," that it has near-magical powers that will improve your life in ways unknown and not yet understood.

Personal branding is post-modern kale that is grown, harvested, and eaten in public—often online.

People who like personal branding understand it isn't optional in the modern age and they usually make that connection innately, at the molecular, DNA level. They don't need to be told to build and polish a personal brand. They just do it, like salmon returning to the same spawning ground each year (if that tributary was Instagram).

To those of you who already believe in the power of personal branding, my message is simple: do not be afraid. There are treasures in these pages. This book will ratify your belief in personal branding and teach you fine points and new techniques that you haven't implemented in the past.

In ways both digital and analog, I've been building my own personal brand since approximately 1994, when I discovered that being smart isn't a viable currency unless you are also consistent and memorable in equal measures. My personal brand is codified and carefully curated to emphasize my few strengths and mask my myriad of weaknesses. I've built multiple companies based—at least in part—on personal branding, and my consulting firm helps companies and executives dig deep on these same issues.

You could say I'm something of an expert on the subject. (Ask anyone!) Yet, I learned A TON from reading *The Road to Recognition*. Seth and Barry give no quarter, pull no punches, and tell no lies. This book is current, useful, and a blast to read. You'll love the exceptional graphics.

So if you're already on board with personal branding, you SHOULD read this book.

But, if you're a denier, a critic, and a cynic of personal branding and/or leafy green superfoods, this is a book you absolutely must read.

The Road to Recognition is not a sermon, treatise, manifesto, or proclamation. The authors are not trying to convince you personal branding is important and then sell you expensive coaching services. They have no skin in the game other than a couple bucks' worth of book royalties and knowing they told the truth and helped some people.

They wrote this book for the right reason: because they've experienced the thesis first-hand and want to share what they've learned with an audience wider than a core group of social media and online marketing fetishists.

They wrote this book because their own lives have been changed for the better (for real, that's not puffery) by personal branding (as has my own).

I'm not suggesting that everyone who reads *The Road to Recognition* will become the best-known expert in their chosen field. For some of you, even after reading this terrific book, you'll think, "I totally get why this is important, but it's not for me. I'm just not comfortable with the whole idea of putting myself out there." And I get that. My wife would rather eat broken glass than think about her personal brand, and even with this scintillating foreword by her betrothed, she wouldn't read this book at the point of a bayonet.

But you will, and I don't even need a sharp, metal object.

And even if you decide to pass when you get to the letter Z, you'll still know exactly why personal branding is as powerful as kale, capable of changing the trajectory of what you're doing day to day, and why the authors and I are so passionate about the topic.

Whether you're a personal branding pro or a personal branding pup, you'll be glad you read *The Road to Recognition*. So get started right now.

Jay Baer
Author of *Youtility* and *Hug Your Haters*
President of Convince & Convert

PREFACE 1
I'm Barry Feldman. And you are?

It's fitting to begin this book with a letter. *The Road to Recognition* uses the alphabet as a narrative device. A is the first point on the roadmap. Z is the last. Simple. Now, back to my letter....

I'm going to give myself a letter grade in personal branding: F.

F is for failure. Yeah, if I'm to look back on my career from a personal branding point of view, I deserve the harsh grade. Why?

I was a laggard. I failed to get serious about developing my personal brand until I was in my 40s. Ironically, I've been writing marketing copy for thousands of brands since I was in my 20s. In the early going, I wrote for chiropractors, contractors, and all sorts of personal brands.

But I neglected mine. I was simply trying to make a living as an advertising copywriter, satisfied with the anonymity of the vocation. There was rarely a day (okay, there was never a day) when I woke up and said, "Today's a great day to develop my personal brand."

Guess what, my friend?

Today is the best day to develop your personal brand. Not tomorrow. Today.

I suppose I didn't realize I was lagging in the ways of personal branding. The term might have been tossed around a bit, but it wasn't a course offered in school, the subject of books, or anything more than an idea slightly ahead of its time muttered by the likes of author Tom Peters and echoed occasionally by eclectic business writers.

Even when personal branding began to gain some traction, I came around slowly. I had a website for fifteen years before I began blogging. I reluctantly joined LinkedIn so as to not be left out. I got going in social media just a few years ago. Podcasting's a new pursuit.

I'm mostly pleased with what I've been able to accomplish in a short time. When I search my name on Google, I like what I see. I've created a sizable digital footprint. I've established a reputation. I'm recognized in the field of digital media and marketing.

Still, I wish I started much earlier. The truth is, publishers don't throw book deals at me. There's no line outside my door of event organizers waiting to pay me to keynote big conferences. And even though I now write for many high-profile websites and blogs, get interviewed often, and land a few spots at the podium, these gigs seldom fall in my lap.

I make them happen. I make connections and ask for opportunities that help build my brand and forward my career. Sometimes I'm rejected; sometimes I'm welcomed. It's not the steep climb it once was, but it's far from an easy ride on cruise control. It's work.

Personal branding is an ongoing class in the school of continued professional education. It's a learning experience, which we're about to share with you.

This book began (unknowingly) about two years ago when I had the idea to create an infographic called *The Complete A to Z Guide to Personal Branding*.

Seth, whom I had collaborated with before, agreed to work on it with me. Seth guided the design and is the reason the graphic went viral. He promoted the hell out of it, pitching it to publishers relentlessly. He repurposed it as a SlideShare and gave it a wider set of wings.

While I did the occasional interview or talk on personal branding, the A to Z Guide was in my rear view mirror. But not Seth's. Sharing personal branding lessons had become a bit of an obsession for my co-author. He created an amazing website entirely focused on personal branding. He made some big plans.

Then he called to tell me about them. Seth declared these lessons shall become a book. He said (or was it threatened?) he'd create it with or without me. So we did this thing together—me with the "I'll get to it when I can" attitude, Seth with the whip.

I wrote the copy for that infographic in a few hours. I simply tossed my ideas down following my instincts, drawing from experience, and sharing ideas I had picked up from Michael Hyatt, Dan Schawbel, William Arruda, and Karen Kang (all authors of inspired personal branding books).

This book was no high-speed affair. We've been bouncing ideas around, writing chapters, collaborating on the design, changing and making up our minds, and scheming launch and promotional plans for nearly two years.

The Road to Recognition could be 26 books. Each chapter covers a big and important topic. And each topic actually is the focus of business books. Our aim is to give you the skinny on each—the need-to-know stuff that'll rev your engine.

I want this book to have a profound affect on your career (and thousands more). I want you to learn from my mistakes, gain from my experience, and above all, I want you to get to work.

How about it? Ready to rally? Ready to rock? Awesome. Let's roll.

Barry Feldman

PREFACE 2
I'm Seth Price. Can I help you?

The Road to Recognition could be the story of a personal journey to take control of one's destiny. In many ways it is. But it's more than that. It's a modern-day toolkit, one that I've used to navigate the digital world, build the career of my dreams, and help countless others to do the same.

My upbringing was hardly storybook. I grew up the latchkey son of a young divorced father. I started working at eight years old. I dropped out of high school to go to college, dropped out of college to start a business, became a chef, entrepreneur, executive, and at times, a leader. I'm telling you this because personal branding was instrumental to my survival.

But this book isn't about me. It's about achieving success in the age we live in.

There is no singular path anymore, no great idea that doesn't require promoting, no guaranteed career, no diploma that will ensure success.

The concepts here are not new. In fact, many can be found in blog posts all over the web. You may have even utilized some of these ideas during your journey to where you are today.

What is new is the focus on creating a roadmap to follow, a coach whispering in your ear the things you need to do to set yourself up for success as you choose your own adventure.

This isn't personal branding theory for marketing geeks. God knows the world has enough of that. This is an actual roadmap for everybody else: the makers and doers of the world.

When it comes to building your brand, it's a jungle out there. Between blogging, social media, networking, websites, content marketing, landing pages, email, and PR, there's so much to manage in today's always-on, always-connected universe.

Whether you're an entrepreneur, student, consultant, artist, yoga teacher, designer, chef, photographer, or retiree, you are a brand with a reputation to be recognized. There's no reason to leave that to others' control.

This book was created to help you cut through the noise and guide you to personal success with organized tips and tactics, clearly outlined in every chapter.

We focused on making the book easy to read and beautiful to look at, simplifying complicated concepts to remove the fluff and jargon that often get in the way of an idea being truly actionable and useful.

I have held every "go-to-market" responsibility imaginable in growing four multimillion-dollar businesses from the ground up—in industries as varied as hospitality, Internet security, real estate, and digital marketing. I've slept on the floor in the office, in the rental car before meetings, at the airport, and on the mats after cleaning the kitchen.

There is no substitute for hustle, but there is a path that has been well worn by the success of many others before you. It's *The Road to Recognition* in the age of digital media.

This road is yours. Buckle up and drive.

Seth Price

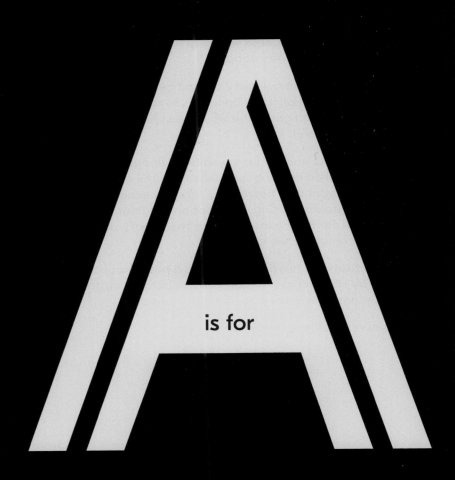

is for

Authenticity

Understand your brand's all about the real you

You, my friend, are a brand. Anything other than the real you won't do. Discover exactly what makes you fascinating. Build your brand on your true strengths and allow it to navigate your road to recognition.

KIM GARST

AUTHOR OF *WILL THE REAL YOU PLEASE STAND UP*

FOUNDER OF BOOMSOCIAL

When you know what the key message of your brand is and what your brand promises to its customers and prospects, it is easy for you to bring this message to the world with a great deal of confidence, no matter what media you are using.

Frankly, it also takes a lot less energy to be

authentic. When you are authentic, when what you are doing matches what you promise, it doesn't feel false and you don't spend energy worrying about how to appear more genuine to your audience. You just are genuine to your audience.

Authentic passion energizes. When you feel passionate, you can't help but take action. It becomes a natural outpouring of what you believe in and what you feel you must do. It is what drives you.

A is for Authenticity

You might think buying this book is the first step in your personal branding journey. Think again. You already have a personal brand. So let's not pretend you're about to create it. The best you can do is develop it, ideally, with purpose and passion.

If personal branding is a road (as the book's title suggests), your challenge is to steer. "Brand" is a tricky thing to describe. In the classic marketing world, most companies try hard to define their brand when, in reality, the market, or more specifically the audience, defines it.

We'll dive deeper into a working definition in Chapter D, but let's start with this. The brand is:

- The impression formed when the brand's name is read or said
- The sum of the experiences a person has had with the brand
- Reputation
- How people describe the brand (not how the company, or person, describes him or herself)

All of the above applies to your personal brand. You don't "spin" your personal brand. You live it. It's what's true about you.

When you achieve success with your personal brand, people recognize you as a specialist. For example:

AJ specializes in helping entrepreneurs use marketing automation to sell information products online.

BJ is a life coach who works one-on-one with CEOs to help them avoid burnout and depression from workaholism.

CJ creates personalized gifts for children designed to foster their love of learning.

DJ is an executive who evangelizes ride sharing as a means to reduce car dependence in crowded cities.

Bring who you are to what you do

Who are you? The core of your personal brand is the person you are, the things you believe in, and the gifts you aim to share. Though many of the platforms you'll use to drive down *The Road to Recognition* will be digital, in personal branding there's no virtual reality.

Authenticity is your key to:

- Build a trusted identity
- Elevate and substantiate your brand in a competitive market
- Set expectations
- Be easier to understand and relate to
- Encourage engagement with like-minded individuals
- Turn audiences into advocates.

At its core, being authentic means staying true to who you are, what you do, and those you serve. I'm not talking about sharing every thought you've ever had but, rather, connecting with people on a human level, as you would with someone you care about.

Let's face it: trust is a valuable but rare commodity. Marketing—the action or business of promoting and selling products or services—generally poses a threat to authenticity and thus, trust. Marketing encourages us to be cynical.

Brand building lures us all into positioning ourselves in the best light, often omitting anything that might harm our image. The urge to woo trumps the inclination to be true. But given the information tools we now have, what's true shall be discovered.

Be true. Be able to say with confidence you are being real, consistent, accountable, thoughtful, and honest. It'll feel right.

Nurture your authenticity

You are unique. This book dedicates pages to exploring your uniqueness. However, you don't need to be unique to be authentic. The definition of authentic is, in a word, "genuine."

Authenticity isn't quite like many of the skills in this book, which can be taught. However, it's something you need to examine and nurture. The process begins by identifying your skills, strengths, talents, values, and passions.

Here are some practical ideas:

Identify authentic people in your niche—Look at role models in your niche. Dig into the content they publish. Why does it resonate with you? What do they do to earn your trust?

Tune into what people say about you—Your friends, family, and mentors can help get you in touch with your authentic self. Get input from them. How do they perceive you? How do they describe you? What strengths of yours do they acknowledge?

Scope your skills—Attempt to identify and document your essential skills. Which do you most enjoy using? Which apply best to your career goals? Make a list of five or more.

Buck conformity—Public enemy number one in personal branding is fear. A fear of being different compels people to conform. Buck it. Let your opinion be known. Set your personality free.

Re-examine your content—As you turn the pages of this book, you're going to begin learning how the things you write and the content you create are expressions of your brand. Don't edit yourself out of it. Infuse your personality into all your communications.

Be clear about your mission—Share it with gusto, but take care to make only promises you know you can keep. Practice what you preach.

Be consistent—Each and every conversation—online and off— is an opportunity to demonstrate your values. Align everything around them and send a consistent message.

Let authenticity be your compass—Throughout this book, you will discover many tips, tactics, and strategies to strengthen your personal brand. Let authenticity help you navigate and develop a brand you believe in.

Are you feeling good about what the real you has to offer? Great. Let's look at how you share it with the world.

is for

Blog

Build your personal brand with a blog

Publish your point of view. The most important personal branding development in the age of digital media is the power to publish at will and express your ideas. Start a blog and keep building on it.

BRIAN CLARK

FOUNDER AND CEO OF
RAINMAKER DIGITAL

You want to be the name that pops in a person's head when a certain area of expertise is mentioned.

Business people have been writing articles for trade publications for decades in order to become niche experts. That's why blogging for business is such a no-brainer, as long as you realize that the content you create is a launch pad for other opportunities that build your brand.

One important caveat, however: focus on delivering value to others and less on self-promotion. You'll find you end up with much more, because people won't care about you until you've given them a reason that transcends you.

B is for Blog

Everything you do online shapes your personal brand. And most, if not all, of your online communications connect back to your blog.

When you're done with this book, you'll have many tools in your personal branding arsenal. Some are more important than others. Some are optional. Blogging is not. Blogging is an imperative discipline of the personal brander.

If you haven't begun blogging, you'll gain some useful starting points here. If you blog now, use the tips here to improve your blog. You should strive to become a better blogger each and every time you go into your content management system and click "new post."

What's the point?

As a business blogger, you're bound to have a number of objectives. How you prioritize them will inform your publishing strategy. Let's examine some of the goals you can work toward with your blog.

Establish authority
Your blog is the hub of your personal branding efforts, where you share your expertise to establish authority in your niche.

Connect with readers
By sharing useful, relevant information, you'll connect with customers, partners, other bloggers, and every conceivable constituent in your social and business circles.

Win business
The majority of brands that blog acquire more customers.

Inspire your social media
You'll promote your blog posts regularly and take advantage of the amplification social networks can provide.

Increase reach
Your blog will be shared and find new eyeballs daily.

Grow your email database

Your blog should inspire people to sign up for your email newsletter list, which, in turn, feeds traffic to your blog.

Generate publicity

As previously mentioned, business bloggers establish authority. When you demonstrate you know your niche, you'll get asked for interviews frequently.

Give your brand a voice

A blog is your pulpit, your publication, your journal—the place where you talk about whatever you choose, however you choose.

Exchange ideas

Blogs obliterate the wall that once stood between a brand and its customers. Encourage interaction, comments, and feedback.

Get (and stay) customer focused

By blogging, you'll learn how to speak in your customers' terms and grow more in touch with your audience's wants and needs.

Increase focus

A subtle addendum to the point above: blogging consistently forces you to define who you are trying to reach and why.

Discover

You are going to learn a lot about yourself and the world around you. It comes with being a writer.

Start with a basic publishing plan

As a business blogger, you become an online publisher. Your starting point is to document a concise plan to address the fundamental why, who, what, and where questions.

Why will you have a business blog?

Establish your goals by considering the ideas above and create a short list that addresses your specific objectives.

Who's the blog for?

Create a persona (or multiple personas) to describe a prototype reader. Include both demographic and psychographic details. The goal is to develop a clear understanding of what pushes the reader's buttons, intellectually and emotionally.

What will the blog offer?

How will your content satisfy the needs of its readers?

Where will it be published?

Your personal brand blog should not be published only offsite, that is, on platforms such as Blogger.com, WordPress.com, Tumblr, Medium, LinkedIn, etc. You may want to take advantage of these channels; however, your interests are best served by hosting a blog on your own domain.

After considering each issue above, document a brief mission statement to define what you will publish, for whom, and the specific value of the content.

Develop a strategic editorial plan

Your business blog needs to focus on specific topics but be broad enough to allow you to perpetually create new and useful content. Let's get into some practical approaches for identifying topics and extracting ways to use them to publish relevant content regularly.

ID the questions prospects ask

You need to discover your prospects' interests, concerns, and challenges and interpret them as questions. What would they type in a search query?

Your prospect's questions might be uncovered in chat, email, phone calls, blog commentary, etc. Tune in closely to these channels and document the questions you're able to gather.

Also, spend time on the social media channels your prospects use. Look for questions and conversations about business challenges. Make and maintain a list of them. You're going to answer them on your blog.

Swipe ideas

Get in the habit of reading the content published in your niche: in blogs, social media, and books. When you discover something promising, document it. Of course, you don't want to plagiarize headlines or copy, but you want great ideas to inspire yours. Create a "swipe file" of inspiring ideas.

Monitor your market

Stay plugged into what's going on in your field. You can keep tabs on industry news with alerts, feeds, and media monitoring tools.

Extend ideas

Don't let a big idea be a singular idea. Use mind mapping apps, a whiteboard, flip chart, sticky notes, or whatever you prefer to brainstorm subtopics and ideas that relate to the core idea and build a bigger story.

Ask your readers

Ask your readers how you can publish content that will help them succeed. You can do this via email invitations to surveys, with on-site survey tools, through groups and forums, and, yes, in conversation.

Log your ideas

When you start blogging regularly, creative ideas will come at you constantly. You can't get to them all immediately. Archive them. Whether it's with a notepad, computer, cloud-based app, or recorder, summarize the idea to the point where it will make good sense when you return to it.

Publish an interesting mix

I believe a great blog delivers variety. This section offers ideas to vary the content of your blog to make it interesting to more people.

- **How to posts**—The "how to" post is the most common style because it's so well received. Deliver valuable insights on how to accomplish something more effectively, and you're bound to produce magnetic posts.

- **List posts**—List posts work. Create them often.

- **Resources posts**—Resources posts aim to enlighten readers by listing helpful books, blogs, shows, products, services, apps, or any type of resource.

- **Roundups**—A roundup is a resource post, but instead of pointing readers to resources, you pull the resources into your story. A popular example is a post where an expert panel is asked the same question.

- **Interviews**—Interviews are great for bringing various points of view and personalities to your blog. You might vary the form by presenting written, audio, and video interviews.

- **Stories**—Storytelling takes practice, so start small. Open with an anecdote, prediction, flashback, a conversation you heard, a joke, whatever. Your stories will get richer and more personal, and your blog will get more interesting.

- **Contrarians**—Take a contrarian stance now and then. Tackle myths, mistakes, and misconceptions. Express your stance.

- **Curation**—Curation is presenting the works of others. It doesn't mean your brain gets to go on vacation. Put some effort into it. You can tee-up favorite stories with an explanation of why you like them. Roll a collection of ideas together to support a story you want to tell. Present opposing views.

- **Reviews**—Be a voice of authority and an industry curator by reviewing books or any form of media. Review anything you deem relevant and potentially useful.

- **Guest posts**—Invite guest bloggers to contribute to your blog. When you make friends on your blogging journey, offer to trade guest posts. Or find someone with writing chops who would welcome the opportunity to find a new audience.

Writing tips for your blog

Most blogs don't accomplish much. They're uninspired and boring. The writing's often forced and phony.

As the hub of your personal brand, you can't allow your blog to be heartless. You don't need to be an exceptional writer, but you must bring passion and originality to your writing. Work at it. Experiment. Gather feedback. You'll learn what does and doesn't work.

Here are some tips to put you on the path to becoming an increasingly effective blogger:

Learn from experienced bloggers
Identify a short list of blogs and bloggers who appeal to you and make a deliberate attempt to understand why. Is it the writing style? The depth? Honesty? Humor? Wit? Sarcasm? Emulate stylistic ideas from some of your favorites. Your style will begin to emerge.

Write several headlines
The headline or title of your post is the most important line you'll write. Put ample effort into making it great. Don't settle for your first idea. When your post comes together, revisit the headline you first wrote and write five to ten alternatives. You'll likely arrive at a stronger one.

Identify with the reader in your lead
After your headline, your lead or opening is the most important passage and must draw the reader in. Communicate to the reader why your post is going to be meaningful. Arouse curiosity about what's to come.

Writers tend to stare at their screens obsessing over the lead for too long. If this problem plagues you, skip the lead and start writing. Your first sentence or paragraph may become much easier after you get a first draft down.

Teach, don't preach
Avoid making your blog a heavy-handed attempt to advertise your products. Adopt an educator's mindset to win your readers' trust.

Have a point of view
Are you concerned some readers won't love what you have to say? Say it anyway. It's not a popularity contest. Write what you feel. Great bloggers share their opinions and present a strong point of view.

Write naturally
Nothing is more tedious than a blogger posturing as a journalist. Relax. Lighten up. Be yourself and write in your natural voice.

Be transparent
Write with uncompromising integrity and don't be afraid to address real issues, problems, and challenges. Tackle the tough questions.

Increase your word power
Powerful blog headlines and copy feature powerful words. I'm not talking about big words. I'm talking about words that trigger emotions. Review your drafts looking for opportunities to tighten your copy, inject active verbs, and dramatize your story.

Make it easy on the eyes
Most readers are skimmers. Use short paragraphs, line breaks, white space, subheads, and lists to make your posts look inviting and maintain interest. Include images and captions.

Give it rhythm
Short sentence. Short sentence. Boring, right? On the other hand, when you run on and on and on with ideas that could be broken up, you run the risk of making reading a chore. Strive to give your writing rhythm. Pacing's important.

Cite research and data
Use the web as your library. Put some effort into enhancing the credibility of your posts with research and data that supports your story.

Respect grammar
Blog posts don't need the approval of a professor. Understand what does and doesn't abide by grammatical standards, but don't be afraid to bend the rules in the interest of style. Just don't embarrass yourself with careless grammar.

Proofread
You'll benefit from a second set of eyes. If an editor or proofreader is not an option, step up your own internal

review system. For spelling, try proofreading your posts backwards—yes, one sentence and word at a time. It also helps to incubate your posts, that is, let them lie for a day or more and return with fresh eyes. Far fewer mistakes will slip by.

Have fun
Don't be stiff and formal and in the habit of cramming useless jargon into your posts. Allow yourself to have fun with the writing.

Make an ask
Like any piece of marketing communications, you should conclude with a call to action. When you've succeeded in taking your reader on a journey you'll want to be a good tour guide and suggest a next step: subscribe, download, read, share. Your options are many.

Stay consistent
The top reason bloggers fail is they simply stop blogging. Establish a reasonable release schedule (it doesn't have to be daily or even weekly) and stick with it. It takes time to build an audience. You need to keep at it.

is for

Content

Create content to connect with your target audience

Valuable content has magnetic power.
On your blog—or in addition to it—create an interesting mix of content in various formats to earn the mindshare and trust your brand needs.

JOE PULIZZI

FOUNDER OF CONTENT MARKETING INSTITUTE

AUTHOR OF *EPIC CONTENT MARKETING*

My personal content creation is everything to my brand. I'm defined in the marketplace by the content that I've created and shared. This started with a consistent blog (back in 2007), then four books starting in 2009, then my posts on LinkedIn and Entrepreneur, and finally (and maybe most important) my speaking content.

All of this has led to building an audience of subscribers over time that we've leveraged in building a sustainable business model. Over time, I've evolved it from just being "Joe's personal brand" to "Content Marketing Institute" where I can leverage my personal brand but it's not necessary anymore for success. I think that should be the goal of every content creator... to build something bigger than themselves.

C is for Content

I'm considering hiring you. I do a search for your name. There you are: your website and blog, your social media profiles, maybe more. What I'm about to see when I click—your content—is going to make some sort of impression on me.

Your brand is largely defined by the content you create and publish.

As such, *The Road to Recognition* is largely about content creation. The previous chapter was about blogging, a cornerstone strategy for most personal branders. Many of the chapters that follow focus on additional areas of content marketing. And most of the other chapters focus on strategies to enhance the success of your content because it's a mainstay of your personal brand development.

Bottom line: the content you offer conveys to the world what you stand for and demonstrates where you can create value. It reveals who you are professionally. "Our online words are our emissaries. They tell our customers who we are," writes Ann Handley in her great book, *Everybody Writes*.

The term "thought leader" has come to mean a person of influence—a trusted expert. Identify the thought leaders in your niche, or any niche. Unsurprisingly, they're the best content creators.

Investing in content is investing in your career

Content marketing is essentially publishing valuable content to attract and engage a targeted audience. It's been ridiculously hot for a decade and it's impossible to fathom it will change anytime soon. Nearly every brand aiming to build their business via digital channels produces content of some sort. You must do the same. Why? Because your content:

- **Showcases your skills**—You put your knowledge on display and make it accessible.

- **Attracts an audience**—Content is discovered via search, social and other channels.

- **Engages your audience**—Great content gets people interested in you and can start a conversation.

- **Increases your reach**—When your content is easy to access and inspired, it's often featured by other content creators and shared.

- **Fuels your social media presence**—Your content is the focus of what you share via social media channels.

What should you create?

A blog is a smart place to start, but it's certainly not your only option and it may not suit you. Let's explore your content creation options now. For starters, I'll present a short list of what people are looking for from content:

- Education

- Entertainment

- Inspiration

The best content delivers a combination of two, or all, of the above. Let's move on to how people consume content:

- Read

- Look at

- Listen to

Again, you have the option to use them separately or in combination. A multi-media approach will often improve engagement.

Now here's a list of popular content formats:

- Blog post

- Article

- Infographic

- Video

- Podcast

- Case study

- eBook

- Book
- White paper
- Webinar
- Event
- Slideshow
- Newsletter
- Quiz or assessment
- Image

This list is long, but hardly complete. Content types continue to proliferate and are only limited to your imagination. The different types or styles of content you can create is long too:

- Guide
- Tutorial
- List
- Tool
- Template
- Story
- Opinion
- Review
- Interview
- Roundup
- Research
- Portfolio

So what content should you create? Consider this equation based on the lists I've offered:

Content Goal + Content Format + Content Style = X

X has endless possibilities. I don't know there is a perfect way to solve for it. You need to research the needs and behaviors of your audience, market and competition. You'll likely form some hypotheses—or hunches. Then you experiment (keeping an eye, of course, on your results).

Begin with something in your comfort zone. Say you're a chef. Your formula might be:

- **Educate/eBook/Tutorial**—A free cookbook as a PDF makes sense.
- **Entertain/Video/Review**—A video of someone who's tried your recipe and wants to comment on it might work.
- **Inspire/Images/Portfolio**—Food is nice to look at. Here's an opportunity to create a collection of food photos from your kitchen.

You get the idea. You have a lot of choices and will only know what works best by trying different tactics. Most businesses actually use more than ten tactics. You need not try to meet or exceed this or any number, especially if you're just getting started with your personal branding, but taking a diverse approach to content creation is likely to prove useful and help you fine-tune your strategy over time.

Make your content great

It's easy to create mediocre content. And most do. They find something that's performing well and create a copycat version. It seldom works. Amongst the oceans of content, the me-too stuff fails to make a ripple.

But don't get me wrong. I'm not saying "don't go there" if the topic you want to tackle is a popular one. In fact, you should. What I am saying is you need to make your content better than the best that exists now. Like most things, to do something remarkable, you need to put extra effort into it.

The book you're reading is a content project, a large one. While its purpose is to help you understand the most effective personal branding tactics, your authors, Seth and Barry, have a personal branding agenda. We aim to be perceived as experts on the topic of personal branding.

Are we offering you insights into a subject no one's yet touched on? Don't we wish? But the topic's red hot. What we're trying to do is create the best possible resource and make it unique, not by way of its topic, but in the ways we've produced and packaged it.

One lesson you can take from this is quality trumps quantity in content creation. One-hit wonders usually won't achieve their goals. You accomplish more by creating less content that's spectacular than you will with volumes of par-for-the-course stuff.

Here are ten more strategies you should apply to make your content great:

Purpose
Make sure your content serves a very clear purpose for the reader/viewer/listener. Avoid being abstract or oblique. Determine what you're trying to accomplish and nail it.

Relevance
Your content must address the reader's pain and/or help bring them pleasure. It should enhance their life at work, at play, or in some way. Develop extreme empathy for your audience to help make your content consistently relevant.

Emotional triggers
Don't make the mistake of believing your readers rely only on rationale to make decisions. It's what we feel that drives our decisions. Great content trips the reader's emotional triggers.

Truth
There's a dreadful amount of conjecture flying around the web which threatens credibility. Backup the points you make with research, facts and quotes you can cite to authoritative sources.

Ease
Ease of access, understanding and readability are all-important to those that consume your content. Compose written content that is easily skimmable and be concise and on-point with your audio/visual content.

Original
Make your content uniquely yours. Even if you're trodding in common territory with content on a popular topic, bring your point of view and voice to the table.

Headline
Content rule number one: thou shalt aim to arouse the reader with a magnetic headline or title. If it fails to create curiosity and interest, it'll be the only line that's read. Write several titles in an attempt to arrive at one that's irresistible.

Shareable
Make it easy for your audience to do you the favor of sharing. Display share bars that are easy to find and use. Feed readers suggestions and shortcuts for sharing your content and ask them to share it. Thank them when they do.

Optimized
The best way to expand your audience over the long haul is to earn a spot on page one of search. Optimize your content for search engines by using keywords and applying SEO tactics. (More to come in chapters G and K.)

Call to action (CTA)
What do you want readers, viewers or listeners to do? Determine this. Tell them where to go, how to get there, and why.

Think broadly, execute narrowly

A topic related to content marketing that's finally getting the attention it deserves is promotion and distribution. Together, you can think of them as reach. A chapter about the effective use of content would be incomplete if it didn't broach the subject. Three important lessons follow, intended to help you maximize the reach of your content.

Think big

Big content takes on deep subjects in detail. Of course, creating it requires more time or money, but it can and should be a smart investment. Not everything you create needs to fall into the "big content" bucket, but some should.

Again, I offer this book as an example. It's about a big topic. It also contains many subtopics (such as the subject of this chapter) that are big content topics themselves. You may not want to write a long business book at this moment in time, but think about how you might take on a big, juicy topic related to your area of expertise that has the potential to be "chapterized" and the legs to take you far.

Repurpose your content

Most of the content you create for a single medium can be re-imagined and re-applied in other media. Apply the idea of repurposing content first to media types. For instance, your eBook can be a series of blog posts. A blog post might make a good infographic or podcast.

Secondly, apply the repurposing strategy to create a larger digital (or even physical footprint) for the same or similar content. You might:

- Offer PDFs or printed copies of written content.
- Create videos for your YouTube channel and publish on your blog or elsewhere.
- Turn a list post into an infographic or slide show.
- Recreate a recorded interview as text-based content.
- Roll several pieces of content into one larger work.
- Use existing content as the basis for webinars.
- Offer written content for syndication elsewhere or update it for publication on an industry blog.

The possibilities for content repurposing are immense. Doing it purposely, and well, can vastly increase your mileage and ROI.

Promote your content

You want to find ways to get your content out there, earn more eyeballs, and generate buzz. There are tons of strategies for doing so, but in an effort to not turn this chapter into a book itself, I want to simply close by advising you to capitalize on the investment you make in creating content by sharing it vehemently across social channels and promoting it online and off in as many ways as you can.

"ALL OF US NEED TO UNDERSTAND THE IMPORTANCE OF BRANDING. WE ARE CEOS OF OUR OWN COMPANIES: ME INC. TO BE IN BUSINESS TODAY, OUR MOST IMPORTANT JOB IS TO BE HEAD MARKETER FOR THE BRAND CALLED YOU."

—TOM PETERS

THE ROAD TO RECOGNITION

is for **Design**

Design a smart and stylish identity

Look good. Everything you create should be presented with class and continuity. Develop a tasty logo, color palette, and design standards that reflect well on your brand.

RICHARD MOROSS
FOUNDER & CEO OF
MOO.COM

Design is a powerful visual storytelling tool. The many, sometimes tiny, choices we make in the visual representation of ourselves or our businesses all add up to how we will ultimately be perceived by others. It can be very subtle, but choosing Helvetica over Gotham in your logo, website, or business card font will transfer some subliminal messaging about what you or your business is about.

Design can play the role of body language for your brand, conveying confidence, style, competency, or professionalism. Great design complements or enhances the true human story behind a brand and provides a shorthand for the recipient to quickly "get" what you stand for and how you operate.

Design is all about the details and, as the founder of a design-led business, it's no surprise that obsessive design thinking is rife in both my personal and professional worlds: from the design of my home, to my wardrobe, even to how I pack a suitcase or organize my email.

D is for Design

According to Seth Godin, a brand is the set of expectations, memories, stories, and relationships that, taken together, account for a consumer's decision to choose one product or service over another.

A brand might also be defined as:

- A perceived image and emotional response to a company, product, or person

- What a prospect thinks of when hearing your brand name

- What people say it is

I'll buy all of these definitions. They all help contribute to an important point: a brand is not a logo. Nor is a brand simply a name or slogan. A brand is much more.

However, we humans (with the gift of sight) are visual creatures. A majority of the information we gather—and recall—is received through our vision. For better or worse, our first impressions are largely formed via visual stimuli.

So despite the fact that your brand represents a myriad of things and is a holistic experience that extends beyond simply peering at a business card or page, there's no denying the making of an effective personal brand requires purposeful design.

You need to look like a pro

Graphic design gives you power to influence how your brand is seen and perceived. You may have the graphic skills you needed to craft the right image for your brand. You may not. Few do. In either case, you'll want to take a serious look at the following design considerations and execute accordingly.

Logo

Your logo will serve as a foundational element of your brand and identity. It will be applied in all the content you create. Your logo, like every element of your brand, should reflect your authentic personality and ideals.

Color

Color carries great psychological power, so it's not to be dismissed as trivial. The color choices you make impart specific emotions and feelings. As a rule of thumb, develop a color palette consisting of just two or three colors to keep your designs clean and simple.

Fonts

Also, create a font palette and try to abide by it. Like you would with your color scheme, select only a few fonts. Consider having a primary pair of fonts that contrast and complement each other.

Photography

Selfies are fun. They have their place, but not in your brand identity. If you're taking your personal branding seriously (and why else would you be reading this book?), you need a high-quality photo you'll use everywhere.

You don't need to be formal about it, but it should not feature your family, friends, or pets (however lovable they may be). Nor should you treat your professional profile picture (you might call it an "avatar") as a place to express your wild and creative self. It's an important part of your digital "hello." Look approachable and professional.

- Make your photo a close-up headshot.

- Look in the camera as you would look someone in the eyes and smile.

- Refrain from filtering or editing the photo.

- Just be you.

What do you do with all your good looks?

I'm glad '"D" appears early in our alphabetical list of the elements of personal branding because, all too often, design becomes an afterthought. You should think about it early and in every project that involves visual elements. That list might include your:

- Business card

- Stationery

- Signage
- Ad premiums/swag
- Collateral
- Packaging
- Website and blog
- Social media cover pages and profiles
- Electronic documents
- Email

Help is available

Many tools and online services make it easier than ever before to tackle graphic design projects. Template-based apps are readily available, which help make your computer, tablet, or even smartphone a powerful platform for design. Photo editors, layout programs, logo design tools, and all kinds of specialty apps can satisfy nearly every need.

Should you decide to enlist the assistance of experienced designers, many online communities (e.g., Fiverr, Upwork, 99 Designs) can connect you to designers for all your needs and with any budget.

A case for consistency

Consistency—or continuity, as marketers say—is enormously important in your branding efforts. Your efforts to select the logo, colors, and fonts that give your brand a "look and feel" quickly fly out the window when they're compromised or violated.

Do an audit of all the places you'll apply your graphic design standards and ensure they're applied across the gamut. Try to make the entire package of design elements—your logo, colors, fonts, images, and designs—become a key part of your brand.

Make your visual identity something to be proud of and your brand easy to recognize at a glance.

"THERE'S A GOOD
CHANCE THA
IF YOU'RE NO
CONTROLLIN
YOUR PERSO

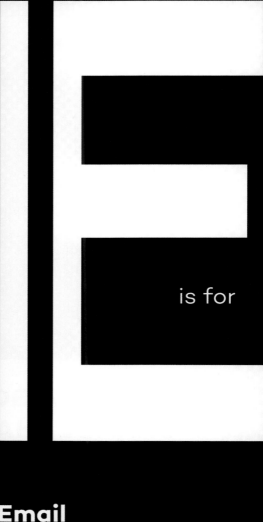

is for

Email

Establish and expand a list of email subscribers

Own an audience. Email is your ace, the money medium. It's private, permission-based, and pervasive. Commit to developing an email list and using it to nurture relationships with your subscribers.

JOANNA WIEBE
FOUNDER OF
CONTENT HACKERS

You must be a friend in the inbox. Maybe you're the funny friend. Maybe you're the trendy friend. Maybe you're the friend with nerdy factoids at your fingertips. Or maybe you're the tough-love friend. Whatever you are, you must be a friend. People don't open emails from brands—personal or corporate—that aren't going to use their time and improve their day like a friend would.

E is for Email

With all the shiny objects flying around the digital marketing space, email marketing is often dismissed as old school, sometimes even unimportant. Kick these notions to the curb right now.

Email marketing is a must for developing your personal brand. Think of how it fits into your day. You probably skip breakfast more often than you skip checking your email. On the receiving end, email generally comes from trusted sources. On the marketers' side, email is the communications tactic where the odds best favor your message reaching its intended destination.

For a variety of reasons, email is the ultimate medium because it's:

- **Permission-based**—Ethical brands send communications strictly to those who grant them permission.

- **Personal**—Email marketing is private and can be personalized specifically for the recipient. You can send the right offer to the right person at the right time.

- **Trust-building**—Email offers a trusted touch point to communicate regularly with readers and nurture the relationship with your friendly voice.

- **Actionable**—Email marketing is a form of direct marketing. Email aims to move the recipient to act.

- **Flexible**—You can play by your own rules and do a lot of different things with email marketing.

- **Accessible**—Email marketing is inherently measurable. You can easily gather insights from your efforts and take action to perpetually improve your results.

- **Easy**—It's not difficult or expensive to master email marketing. Your ROI can dwarf any other channel.

Get set up with an email service provider (ESP)

Unless you want some serious headaches, don't flirt with the idea of creating your own email infrastructure or depending on email software. Your ticket to success with email marketing begins with selecting an email service provider (ESP) because they make it easy to:

- Get started without messing with hardware and software
- Get the highest possible deliverability rate
- Manage subscriber lists
- Build email campaigns
- Gather and review campaign reports

The services are inexpensive, but you have a ton of choices, so consider the following:

- **Design ease**—Look for a robust set of templates and drag-and-drop creation tools that allow you to be creative without design and coding skills or resources.
- **Testing**—Review the ESP's testing features, such as A/B subject line tests.
- **Reporting**—Be sure it gives you easy access to reports that reveal high-level metrics, subscriber information, and performance data.
- **Segmentation**—To send targeted campaigns, you'll need to be able to segment subscribers by variables you choose.
- **Mobile-ready**—The majority of email is now opened and read on mobile devices, so ensure your email is automatically formatted to look great on all devices.
- **Support**—Providers offer various combinations of phone, chat, and email services. Make a choice you're comfortable with and consider the provider's reputation for support.
- **Fees**—Try to anticipate your needs and look into the pricing plans and fees. Most providers offer free trials. For low-volume needs, some even offer free services.

Start building an email list

You need to create and grow an email list. Generally, you build your list through your website by offering visitors some form of valuable content. Digital marketers often refer to such offers as "lead magnets." (See chapter O for ideas on offers.)

There are a variety of effective tactics you can use to collect email addresses:

- **Landing page**—An effective way to capture email leads is on a landing page where your free resource is offered. For optimum conversion, don't make the form you place there "greedy." Request only the information you must know. A name and email address should suffice.

- **Pop-ups**—Pop-ups have become popular and far more accepted than in their early days. They're offered by a slew of services in different of forms with various features.

- **Feature box**—An alternative to the pop-up that might feel less intrusive is the feature box, a row on your web page. It functions like a pop-up but is a permanent fixture.

- **Preview page**—Another approach gaining momentum is the page-dominating preview page (or takeover page). When a new visitor arrives, the first thing loaded is a full-screen landing page that offers a subscription.

- **Dedicated subscription page**—You can dedicate an entire page to encouraging email subscriptions. On the page, you'll describe the benefits of receiving your email. This strategy might be particularly attractive if you don't yet have eBooks or other forms of lead magnets to offer.

- **Sidebar**—Placing a form in the sidebar of your homepage, blog, or anywhere across your website (desktop version only) is a popular convention and is made easy by your email service provider.

We've covered the more popular strategies, but the list goes on. You can build your email list with:

- An offer at the conclusion of a purchase process

- A form on your Facebook page

- A Twitter lead generation card
- Social media ads to lead traffic to a landing page
- A link in your email signature
- A box below (or above) blog posts

And what about offline?

- Use a sign-up sheet at the office, store, or event
- Use a tablet for any of the above
- Include an insert in shipments or invoices with instructions on how to subscribe
- Collect business cards
- Promote email on your business cards and in sales materials

Increase value with list segmentation

Different people on your list are likely to have various interests in the things you offer. Enter list segmentation. The segmentation capabilities most ESPs offer can up your game by enabling you to use subscriber data to create and send targeted campaigns, which uncorks a whole new realm of possibilities for sending triggered or behavior-based email.

Newcomers to email marketing should proceed carefully but, along your email marketing journey, consider the following:

- **Start slowly**—In most cases, keep things simple and just ask for an email, but you can begin building segmented lists per the landing pages and forms used.

- **Offer autoresponders**—You can build more targeted lists by making specific offers that are fulfilled automatically with an email or series of emails.

- **Subscription options**—Give customers the option to get notifications based on their desires. Examples: frequency, subject matter, type of email (newsletter vs. discounts, etc.).

- **Advanced segmentation**—Advanced segments can be created based on purchase history, email consumption, website activity, demographics, and more. You can use any combination of data to define a specific group of customers.

Understand your strategic email options

Here are several ways to tap the power of email:

Newsletters

Newsletters are a way to build trust, nurture leads and foster retention. You put your brand, content, products, services, tips, tactics, and whatever else you choose in front of your prospects and customers at regular intervals. To create newsletters efficiently, you can compile relevant content and news from sources inside and outside your company. Many of the best newsletters feature a steady stream of curated content.

Digests

Digest-style emails are simply lists of content, usually blog posts, though they can include podcasts, infographics, or anything you can click to get. Digests typically include short descriptions of the content and, of course, links.

Autoresponders

An autoresponder is a series of emails—usually focused on a specific topic—and often, a specific persona. Autoresponders are delivered in a predetermined sequence at predetermined intervals.

Welcome email

New subscribers are the most likely people to open your emails. Sending personalized welcome emails creates a connection with first-timers and builds trust. Welcome emails might educate recipients about your value proposition, ask them to tell you more about themselves, and provide resources and helpful information personalized to their interests.

Special occasions

Special occasions can make for special emails. Consider emails to recognize your readers' special occasions: birthdays, anniversaries, holidays, or important milestones in their lives or your relationship.

Transaction emails

You can follow up with transactions of every sort (e.g., order status, shipping notices, or confirmations) with tips, FAQs, invitations to social networks, requests for feedback, and more.

The list goes on, especially for email designed to sell.

- Special offers and discounts
- Invitations to events
- Cart (or form) abandonment
- Re-ordering
- Lapsed purchasing

I believe I mentioned email is flexible. You can mix and match to find the email tactics that meet the needs of your audience, and ultimately, prove effective for your goals. You can mine your data to perpetually improve results. But I don't want to scare you before you begin. In fact, the point I most want to make in this chapter is to begin.

Make email a part of your personal branding strategy starting today.

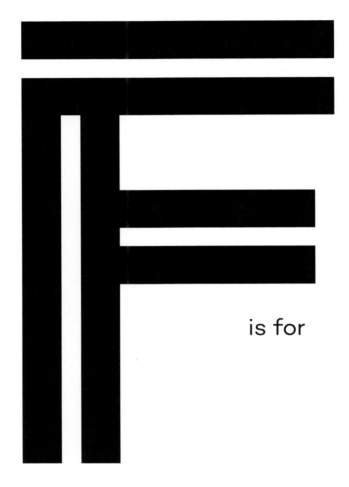

is for

Followers

Grow a following and lead the conversation

New media is a two-way street. You can't have a brand without an audience. Social media makes it possible to develop a tribe of followers— like-minded people with common interests—who you aim to educate and inspire.

JEFF BULLAS
AUTHOR OF *BLOGGING THE SMART WAY*
CEO OF JEFFBULLAS.COM

The core tactic for all marketers and entrepreneurs in a digital world is growing digital media distribution networks. Your followers are a big part of that equation.

On the social web, we all need to think like publishers. Without this, the content will not get the attention and engagement it deserves. Without distribution, content is often hidden in the nooks and crannies of the web and is never seen, heard, or viewed.

My initial tactic to reach the world with my content, get noticed, and build a business was to use Twitter. In the last seven years, I have focused on building a large following and tribe on Twitter, and now we are approaching half-million followers. It has been the difference between anonymity and high global visibility.

F is for Followers

Do you really need followers? The idea sounds vain, doesn't it? In fact, social media marketers often dub "follower" counts (and versions of the word across social media channels, such as likes, fans and connections) a vanity metric.

Get over it right here and now. Yes, you need followers. Why? Because your aim is to lead. You don't need to lead a nation or industry. You need to lead a community of like-minded people.

You can't have a brand without an audience

This simple little slice of the truth is all-important. Your audience can be a handful of people, millions, or more realistically, somewhere in between. The idea is to gain the trust of an audience.

They'll associate you with a specific subject—your subject. They'll count on you for answers. To point the way. To lead.

Seth and I created this book to lead you down an accelerated path to personal brand development. We're not trying to manipulate you. We're trying to help. We want you to think of us when your thoughts turn to a subject called personal branding. We're flattered you're following.

Social media makes it all possible. There may be a million and one ways to build an audience, but there's never been a more powerful one than social media. Of course, millions of pages of social media advice have been published (a small percentage were written by experts), but here and now, we'll try to cover the most essential strategies for building a following.

Start smart and be selective

It can be challenging to master the feature sets of social media networks. They change constantly. You're likely to find it overwhelming if you try to master too many too quickly. We recommend starting slow—with just one or two.

For the development of your personal brand, LinkedIn is a must. Start there. LinkedIn is all about business. Generally speaking, the ever-expanding roster of social channels are not. It'd be tricky for us to prescribe which social networks to join or what order to join them in. If you're producing a steady stream of content, Twitter is the odds-on favorite for your number two network, but a number of variables come into play.

Try to prioritize based on what you can observe about your specific market and audience. Which are the networks where the activity levels are highest? Where do you think you'll make the most meaningful connections for your brand?

Create rich profiles

Every social network requires you to establish a profile page where you're given an opportunity to define your brand. Don't make the mistake of rushing through the process of creating yours. Give careful consideration to positioning yourself as specifically as possible based on your expertise and experience. Select the keywords most likely to get you discovered via search, and while you need to take a professional approach, inject as much personality as possible.

Think visually

Use the same (or similar) profile photos across your social media pages for continuity. Use a consistent color palette too. You want visual cues to create stronger recognition of your personal brand.

Use visual media to your advantage whenever possible, including photos, illustrations, visual treatments of quotes, infographics, and videos. Consistent visual marketing will help you draw more attention to your content and brand.

Follow

Your path to engaging an audience on social media begins by following others. Most social media networks offer suggestions on who to follow based on your profile. Take these suggestions. Also, follow people you know, customers, and influencers in your niche.

The more people you follow, the more followers you'll get. Try entering keywords in the search tool to find people with common interests. Also, consider following those who follow the people you follow. (You follow me?) Most people will follow you back.

Share wisely

Try not to be overly aggressive with any one tactic—such as promoting your content. The most successful people on social media generate interest in their brand and gain followers by sharing a mix of:

- Teasers and links to their own original content
- Highlights from, and links to, credible and relevant content from other sources
- Fun updates and posts that don't promote anything but, instead, aim to inspire conversation

Comment

The heartbeat of social media is conversation. While sharing content can be thoughtful and smart, commentary is better still. Much of the content you come across will provoke thoughts, just like any conversation.

Express yourself

Agree. Disagree. Answer questions. Ask questions. Cite examples. Offer links. Say thank you.

Social media is a conversation. When you put something into it, you get something out of it. Have fun with it and watch your following expand.

Be consistent

Budget time to do social media. You'll be taken far more seriously if you're active on a daily basis. You can take short breaks without threatening your good standing, but if you merely check in now and then, you won't be taken seriously.

Promote like a leader

Let it be known you're active in social media and want followers. Showcase links to your social sites across the gamut of touch points, including your:

- Website
- Online properties (including other social media)
- Email signature
- Newsletter
- Business cards
- Advertising

The number of followers you have is far less important than the quality of your followers. It's been said that you can build an amazing personal brand with 1,000 true followers, and if those followers happen to be influencers, you could probably achieve success with even fewer.

Start today by taking stock of the followers you already have, make an effort to nurture their support, become a fan of their work, and most of all, thank them for being a part of your journey.

THE ROAD TO RECOGNITION

is for **Google**

Assess how the world sees you

Search yourself. Think of Google as the business card the entire world has instant access to. You need to "Google yourself," evaluate the results, and create and execute a plan to look good in the eyes of the searcher.

SUJAN PATEL

CO-AUTHOR OF *100 DAYS OF GROWTH*

CO-FOUNDER OF WEBPROFITS

Google is today's go-to source of information. By leveraging Google to build your personal brand, you get credit for being the source of that information.

There are 3.5 billion searches per day. Why not seize a fraction of that? When I launched my book last year on growth hacking, I leveraged SEO to help me build my brand on all things growth hacking. I did this by writing articles, answering questions on Quora, guest blogging, and creating videos, all just to rank on Google for keywords around the topic of my book.

The result: 27% of my sales in the last year (10,000 book sales) came from Google. I've also been cited on over 54 blogs and publications on topics related to growth hacking. Guess where they found my content? I'll give you a hint: it starts with a G.

G is for Google

Say your name is new to someone—a prospective employer, recruiter, partner, client, writer, or what have you. What web page will they call upon to find your website and social profiles, and learn more about you? You know it. Google.

Ever Google yourself? We encourage you do so now and regularly in the future. A Google search result is the easiest, fastest, and best way to gauge your public persona. Consider the act of searching your name a health status check for your personal brand.

When you get to chapter L of this book, you'll discover our thoughts on LinkedIn, namely, that it's your personal branding epicenter. It's where you present your credentials and more. If LinkedIn is your resume, think of Google as your business card.

But all is not fair on a Google search. Let's look at some ground rules for your personal brand search and discuss how the cards may not be stacked evenly for everybody.

First, understand that Google is wise to your identity, past search behaviors, online preferences, and more. When you search in the default mode, Google will return "private results," and you're bound to get a page of deceptively encouraging hits. Google recognizes you're searching for yourself.

Here are three ways to search Google to get impartial results, like an outsider would:

- Select "hide private results" in your search settings.
- Switch your browser to incognito or private mode. In this mode, your search history should not be a factor.
- Use a web browser you normally don't.

Another factor, which is largely out of your control, is the popularity of your name. As with all search terms, competition looms large. If you should happen to have a very unique name, you're more apt to find some of your web properties on the first page. Conversely, the Joe Smiths of the world have an unfair disadvantage.

Barry Feldman is far from a unique name. As I write this chapter, I'm pleased to tell you you'll find me with every search result on pages one and two of a "public" Google search.

Seth's results are much different. He competes with an artist of the same name who's worked hard to earn page-one real estate.

Clearly, a variety of factors are beyond your control. What else can you do?

If you feel it's early in the game or not too late to revisit your "brand" name, consider a few alternatives to simply branding your first and last name.

- Add a middle initial or middle name.

- Select a modifier that will serve you well. For instance, writer Jeff Goins brands himself as "Goins Writer."

- If you're an entrepreneur, consider using your name and an additional word or two for your company name. For instance, my company is Feldman Creative. Luckily, I have no competition for the name, so searches for it reveal my many social media profiles as well as sites that publish my guest posts.

Do this as well: set up a Google Alert for each brand name you want to monitor. It takes just seconds to tell Google Alerts you'd like to be sent email when your name appears online.

Do you like what do you find?

If you dominate the first page of a Google search as many accomplished personal branders do, you've done well to optimize your online properties. Again, though you can't control everything, you make your own luck here with the actions you take to build your personal brand.

Let's look at some potential listings on the SERPs (search engine results pages). I'll use mine for reference and to help me share some important ideas.

Website and blog

The first two organic listings are my website and blog. This is ideal because these are the two properties over which I have the most control. I decide what does and doesn't get published.

You want to strive to get your website and blog ranked high. In the "K is for Keywords" chapter, we'll cover some search engine optimization (SEO) techniques for accomplishing this. Understand that persistence is required. Google serves pages based on relevance and authority, so you should expect it to take some time to achieve high rankings, especially if you have formidable competition.

LinkedIn profile

You definitely want your LinkedIn profile to be discovered via a Google search. You'll accomplish this by optimizing your LinkedIn profile and actively using it to build your network and publish relevant content.

Other blogs

Guest blogging (contributing articles to publishers in your niche) delivers a massive advantage for search. In fact, of the 20 results presented on pages one and two for a "Barry Feldman" search, seven are either author pages or individual posts I've written.

Snippets for my guest post author page listings are short passages taken from author bios. If you click through, you land on a page with information about yours truly, links to my website and social profiles, and a catalog of my articles published there.

The two websites where I guest blog currently that show up on page one are Social Media Today and HubSpot. Why? (1) I have a strong presence on both, and (2) these websites naturally rank high because they have established immense authority.

Google+

If it were based only on its merits as a social channel, I might not call out Google+. Its strength as a connector is debatable, and the network changes relentlessly. Truth be told, Google+ continues to confuse its members. However, perhaps for obvious reasons, Google gives its own service special treatment.

Even with a limited amount of activity, your Google+ profile could outrank some of your other social media. What's more, Google SERPs often include individual G+ posts when they're relevant. Finally, when people within your Google+ network use Google to search your name, they're likely to be served a rich snippet or Google "business card," meaning the listing presented might include an image, contact information, recent posts, and more details. The actual content presented is based on how you've set up your Google+ preferences.

Other channels

Plod through my search results and you'll find my Twitter, Facebook, About.me pages, quite a few additional blogs I write for, and many pages where I was featured in interviews, spoke at a conference, got mentioned in an article or list.... And so on and so forth.

You dictate what people dig up

I didn't run through the examples above to boast. I did it to show you how a Google search is a conduit to your digital footprint and online persona.

Your results might be less robust. If you're actively creating content and connecting with influential people and publishers, they might be more robust. The channels might differ. You might find you rank on page one for Pinterest or another rising star in social media.

The point is, while you can't control Google search, it's up to you to be found. Searching your name is very telling. It'll tell you where you stand. And it'll tell the outside world not only who you are but what you do, what you make, and what you have to say.

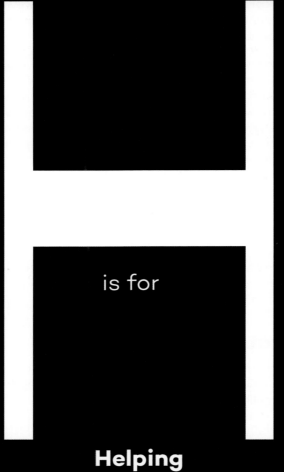

is for

Helping

Offer what you can, whenever you can

Put goodwill to work. Don't wait for opportunities to come to you. Find ways to be helpful. Be the first to volunteer, connect people, or get behind meaningful missions.

There are two types of helpers: those that help others with self-serving expectations and those that simply help. Be the latter.

I wish I was kidding, but I often see people put out press releases after they've done a good deed. Then there are the ones who connect on Twitter or Facebook and follow up immediately with a direct message asking for something. WTF is that?

SCOTT STRATTEN
AUTHOR OF
UNMARKETING

Helping others with your deeds, contributions, and content is a wonderful business practice, so just do it. If you want to win allies and make meaningful connections, don't call in favors. Be generous. You'll get yours.

H is for Helping

LeBron James is a personal brand of epic proportions. Four-time NBA MVP. Three-time champion. Two-time Olympic gold medalist. His fans call him "King James."

Another big name that calls Cleveland home is marketing superstar Joe Pulizzi, author of *Epic Content Marketing* and founder of Content Marketing Institute. Marketers call Joe the "Godfather of content marketing."

People might not line up to get an autograph from Joe to the degree they do LeBron, but you'd be hard-pressed to find someone who's done more to align his personal brand with a niche and benefit from the recognition.

I'm a fan of both the King and the Godfather, but I don't know LeBron. I do know Joe. When I think of him, the first thing that comes to mind is his generosity.

When my personal branding pursuits began to pay off—largely through guest blogging for popular websites—requests started coming at me daily: Will you contribute to my article? Do an interview? Be a guest on my webinar? Share my content? Try my service? Etc.

I was talking to Joe one day at a conference where both of us were speaking. I asked him, "Joe, I'm getting bombarded with requests to help people with this and that. Given your status in the industry, I would imagine you get the same thing to a much higher degree. What do you do?"

Joe's response: "Barry, I try to help everybody I possibly can."

How can I help you?

You've heard this question a million times. How often is it genuine? How often does it come with no self-serving agenda? Rarely. It usually comes from someone who wants something from you. They want to take your order.

If you polled experts on the most important skills for personal branding, there's no doubt the ideas you collected would include ambition, vision, communications, as well as many of the topics covered in this book. Generosity may not make the list. It definitely should.

Giving of yourself—helping others—is a major key to elevating your personal brand. Being generous with your skills and time will catapult your success. Why?

- **Helping others makes you a leader**—True leaders are willing to teach, help others advance, showcase their skills, and learn from others.

- **You activate your network**—Helping others leads to opportunities. You send a message about what it means to be connected to you, and your network is more likely to reciprocate.

- **You grow**—All your interactions have the potential to deliver personal and professional growth. Being helpful proves you are a team player.

What can you offer people?

All of these ideas will help you achieve the benefits presented above—and then some. And you can probably find more opportunities to be helpful.

Offer your time

Time is our most precious commodity. People will notice and appreciate when you offer your time to help them. Consider these ideas:

- **Free consultations**—Make yourself available for consulting calls to prospective clients, students, or anyone.

- **Be a mentor**—Offer to mentor a student or newcomer to your business, or be prepared to respond when someone comes calling for advice.

- **Give to the community**—Donate your skills to a charity, school, or a cause that inspires you.

- **Just say yes**—The more you put yourself out there in the media, the more requests you'll field. Oblige these requests and make the most of them.

Offer your wisdom

You can share what you know in so many ways.

- **Content**—Publishing content is all about delivering your insights. Try to create truly useful content and deliver it free of charge—whether it be a blog, video series, podcast, eBooks, research, or anything else.

- **Guest blogging**—Offer publishers exclusive blog posts and articles.

- **Seminars**—Seize opportunities to teach in classroom settings, workshops, webinars, virtual summits, etc.

- **Social media**—Seek and you shall find infinite opportunities to share your expertise via social conversations, social media groups, forums, Q&A sites, live chats, and more.

- **Answer the call**—As I wrote about earlier, when you're rolling down *The Road to Recognition*, you'll get the call to contribute to others' content in a variety of ways. Do your best to respond to it.

Offer your resources

If you're in a position to create opportunities for others, take advantage of them.

- **Internships**—Can you offer up-and-comers a chance to intern at your company or with organizations you're affiliated with?

- **Place**—You may be able to offer a place—physical or virtual—to bring like-minded people together.

- **Offer your endorsement**—Helping others can be so easy. Just endorse their efforts.

- **Social sharing**—Tweet, pin, like, or share. Tell your fans and followers about interesting or valuable content created by others in your network.

- **Reviews**—Want to help someone who's published a book or makes videos or podcasts? Leave them a positive review. It's easy and meaningful.

Offer your network

Connecting people you know and want to help is one the most meaningful things you can do.

- **Welcome guests**—Aspiring bloggers may want to get published on your blog. Experts may want to be a guest on your podcast, join your webinar series, and speak at your events. Welcome them when you can.

- **Introduce people to each other**—No one forgets the person who introduces them to a potential client, boss, or mate. It's powerful and enormously rewarding. Take time to connect people whose skills or interests complement one another.

We've explored quite a few ways to help others and probably just scratched the surface. The opportunities are infinite. At some point, you may fear they'll tax your time. I'm not saying to never politely decline, but I am saying you'll help yourself by being a giver. No one advances to the peaks of career success without help, and no one stays at the top without being helpful.

is for

Influencers

Look up and connect with the people you look up to

New friends will open doors. Influential professionals have prominent friends. Seek out leaders, surround yourself with them, and find ways to be of value to them.

LEE ODDEN
AUTHOR OF *OPTIMIZE*
CEO AT TOPRANK
MARKETING

When brands want to become more credible and extend their reach, they find people who already have influence and partner with them to create content. The same approach works for individuals. If being more influential in a certain area is important to your success, find people who have the trust, respect, and audience you want.

Study them: Where do they spend time online? What do they say? Who do they engage with and what do they care about? Find out what you can provide those influencers that they are not getting otherwise.

Take a "give to get" approach and empathize to understand where you can create value. Focus on creating a real connection around mutual goals. As you engage with others who are influential, your influence will grow by association.

I is for Influencers

We all want to be influential. You might say personal branding itself is the process of building influence.

The idea isn't so much about feeding your ego (stay humble, my friend), but rather to build authority in your niche. Your goal is to associate your personal brand with a specific topic—your area of expertise—in the minds of your audience.

This chapter focuses on leveraging the authority of others through influencer marketing. In simple terms, influencer marketing can be thought of as the fine art of getting big kahunas in your camp. To achieve greater reach and resonance (pardon the fancy marketing words), you try to win over the people who already have it. You make friends in high places.

One company in the field defines influencer marketing as "a type of marketing that focuses on using key leaders to drive your brand's message to the larger market." They go on to say, "Rather than marketing directly to a large group of consumers, you instead inspire/hire/pay influencers to get out the word for you."

I don't like the "hire/pay" part, although this form of marketing has exploded. Of course, the celebrity endorser falls into this category. You know LeBron James drives a Kia, right?

There's nothing new about that form of marketing, but there's also a booming business going on where bloggers and social stars are bribed, er, compensated, to plug products. For instance, the influential YouTube baking instructor tells you which brand of chocolate chips to use (in exchange for a year's supply of them). The ethics of that form of influencer marketing can be questionable.

The influencer marketing we'll discuss—the type that's appropriate for personal branding—calls for:

- Targeting people your prospects trust for information

- Engaging people who shape the important conversations in your niche
- Achieving kinship with people whose endorsement will forward your personal branding objectives

The process is essentially relationship building

The tactic that goes to work in influencer marketing is word of mouth, the most powerful kind of marketing in any era, market, or media. The process isn't exactly magic, but its effect could indeed be magical.

How do you build relationships with someone who sways opinion? The key is reciprocity. You give first and get later. This powerful principle of persuasion has been taught countless times as a key to building influence.

Our friend Doug Kessler, co-founder of Velocity Partners, states the concept oh so simply. He writes, "If you want an influencer to be a shiny cog in your content distribution machine, be one of the hardest-working cogs in theirs."

See, content marketing and influencer marketing are close friends. It's been said content is the currency of influence.

Tune into your audience
The influencers you want in your camp are accomplished content marketers. The key to getting started is "listening," which, in the world of digital marketing, means reading (of course you may also be playing and viewing multimedia assets).

Focus on what influencers are creating and how the content is received
You're bound to see which topics create the most conversation and sharing. Use your influencers as your content thermometers. Track their work with social media tools, feeds, and Google Alerts. You'll get a feel for what's hot and what's not.

Identify influencers

Which influencers should you target? You probably already know which people are the movers and shakers in your field. They're the speakers, authors, and prominent bloggers.

Social media makes it easy to identify additional influencers. Search social channels by topic to identify people who deliver an attractive combination of relevance and reach. And, of course, you'll want to factor in "resonance," meaning engagement levels. Do they engage with their audience and drive conversions?

In addition to using the social channels separately, you can take advantage of influence marketing tools and platforms. There are too many to mention here, but you'll find it useful to start with BuzzSumo, a tool expressly made to analyze how content performs on social media and search and for identifying influencers.

Join the conversation

When you know who the influencers are—and where they are—next, you want to get on their radar. I've seen the process described as "seeding." You want to plant seeds and nurture them but refrain from asking for anything from influencers in the early going. You can do so in a variety of ways with social media:

- Follow them.
- Share their work.
- Try to engage in social exchanges.
- Comment in blog comment threads. For instance, express your opinion in response to an opinion piece.
- Offer select pieces of your content that are relevant to the conversation.
- Create new content in response to pieces you've seen that started a conversation.
- Write reviews where applicable (such as a book review on Amazon).
- Say "thank you" when your contributions are recognized.

- Write targeted and personal emails.
- Facilitate connections and new relationships amongst influencers and audience members.

These types of activities will not go unnoticed by your influencers. They're influential because they're forever aware of the sentiments of the people they influence.

Collaborative content: the ultimate influencer marketing play

Seth and Barry are often accused of being influential in the digital marketing space. Why? We created content for—and with—marketing influencers. This can be done in many ways:

- **Include their content in yours**—Embed their tweets, pins, and social updates, etc. Quote influencers in your posts. Showcase their media, such as SlideShares, YouTube videos, and infographics.

- **Interview them**—Do a video interview, podcast, written interview, roundup post, or all of the above. Don't be bashful about asking. You may not get 100 percent participation (influencers are busy), but you'll be surprised by the outcome. Influencers enjoy being interviewed and value opportunities to find new audiences (even if they are small).

- **Create roundups**—Roundup posts (or other content types) include ideas from a roster of influencers. You can ask them to participate, or you can simply write about several influencers in one piece. For example: recommended books, blogs, podcasts, or email lists.

- **Create content based on your influencers**—I heard Mr. X speak and... I read Mrs. Y's great book and... I tried Group Z's ideas and... This is all influential stuff.

- **Return all favors**—When you're practicing influencer marketing, your turn will come. You'll be asked to be included or featured in content by others working on developing their personal brands—or even by your influencers. Be 100 percent available and generous.

- **Reach out**—Consider driving the process. Reach out to your influencers when you're confident you have something of value. Some examples:
  - Offer your infographics and presentations.
  - Invite them to be guests on your webinars or interviews.
  - Deliver research you've conducted.

As a result of creating content collaboratively, you'll likely come to know more influential marketers. You'll find yourself welcome in their social circles, and new opportunities will arise. Influencer marketing isn't just reciprocal, it's contagious.

Maintain your momentum

Here are some tips for maintaining the momentum of the content marketing tasks critical to your influencer marketing.

Create an idea file
Use a spreadsheet, a planning calendar, notes, or any tool you prefer to record collaborative content ideas.

Stay positive
Again, influencer marketing is largely reciprocal, and your deeds will mostly be rewarded. When they're not, don't take it personally. Move on. If you're in an attractive and lucrative space, you'll score plenty of meaningful relationships by putting in the effort.

Be helpful
As we stressed in the previous chapter, "Do unto others." Understand how you can be most helpful and get on it.

Make it easy
If you want the cooperation of a busy leader in your field, offer options when asking for something: "We can have a call, chat, email," or "You can point me to a resource of yours if you're tight for time." Don't be difficult or needy.

Keep tabs
Establish a measurement system—formal or otherwise—to help determine whether your efforts are being rewarded or not.

Promote your influencers
Recommend your influencers often. Doing so may compel them to share your content or invite you to become a guest blogger on their website.

Apply patience
Your first roundup, book review, or interview may not drive you from zero to well-known, but you need to be realistic and patient. When roadblocks occur, try other avenues. If you have the chops to pitch your guest blogging services, use this strategy often.

Stay social
Influential people in your industry, especially the content creators, are forever in tune with social media. Don't forget this. Forward their cause.

This book is a lesson in influencer marketing

By now you've noticed every chapter in this book includes a contribution from a writer other than the authors. We asked authors, marketers, and business leaders we respect to give us these passages.

Why? We believe every contributor, many of them friends, adds credibility and depth to *The Road to Recognition*. We trust these people. We value their wisdom. Given their accomplishments, authority, and reach, associating our brand with theirs is immensely helpful.

Simply said, collaborating with influential people has helped give the work we've done greater influence. You can boost your personal brand with influencer marketing too.

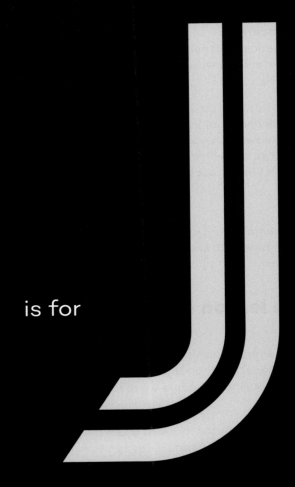

is for

Joining

Join communities where ideas are incubated

Make your way into social circles.
Affiliations are all-important to the growth of your brand. Find groups you'd be proud to be a part of, get involved, and make your presence known.

VANESSA DIMAURO
FOUNDER OF
LEADER NETWORKS

To advance personally and professionally, we need to learn what others have experienced, share what we know, and be a part of something bigger than ourselves.

It's as simple as connecting the dots:

Joining puts us on the path to belonging. Belonging leads to community. Community yields collaboration and knowledge sharing. And collaboration and knowledge sharing drive competitive advantage. That means joining truly is the first step on the path to excellence.

J is for Joining

No doubt you've heard a number of maxims to this effect:

You are the company you keep. You're the average of the five people you spend the most time with. The power of positive thinking is contagious. Two heads are better than one.

Sure, we're bordering on (or even borrowing from) cliché inspirational posters and Internet memes. But rhetoric it's not. It's life on planet togetherness. Joining and participating in groups can be immensely helpful for your career.

That's why professional groups are everywhere. They exist online and off, in all different sizes and for a variety of purposes.

During the writing of this book, Seth and Barry were invited to become members of a private Facebook group for non-fiction writers. Ideas are flying there. Beneficial new relationships are being born.

The infinite benefits of professional groups

While networking is certainly a part of the picture, joining and participating in groups can be beneficial in so many ways. You'll:

- **Be challenged, focused, and motivated**—Groups can help keep you on track, enable you to think bigger, and push you to achieve your goals.

- **Be accountable**—Talking to and working with your peers can challenge you to step up your game. Share your goals with them and ask them to hold you accountable.

- **Get ideas**—The collective power of the groups you join will foster your creativity and problem-solving skills. You're likely to get ideas for projects or even products.

- **Get feedback**—Your peers will give you feedback to continuously help correct your course. Groups create a sense of security and trust.

- **Gain confidence**—Surrounding yourself with like-minded people will serve to support and inspire you. You'll become a better decision maker and increase your confidence.

- **Expand your skills**—Interacting with other members will enable you to pick up new skills and talents.

- **Develop leadership skills**—Professional groups give you an opportunity to develop leadership skills. You may find yourself mentoring others, coaching, and teaching.

- **Help others**—Zig Ziglar said, "You can have everything in life you want, if you will just help enough other people get what they want." You'll find great satisfaction in helping others.

- **Do some good**—Groups tend to pursue worthwhile causes that you'll be able to play a part in or lead.

- **Make friends**—You'll get more opportunities to share your dreams and vision. You'll create deep connections with some great people.

- **Discover new opportunities**—Collaboration opportunities will present themselves often. All kinds of doors may open for you.

Who should you surround yourself with?

Surround yourself with good people. They don't have to be saints. They have to make you feel good. In a post on Inc. com, Janine Popick (friend, client, entrepreneur, and business leader), answered the question in several ways, which are too good not to share.

- **People who love life**—Get into groups and form relationships with people who have a positive attitude. They enable you to think beyond the job, which sometimes gives you more inspiration.

- **People who are really good**—We're not talking about talent; we're talking about people who are good to others, people with heart. These are people you want hang with, talk to, and laugh with.

- **People who challenge you**—People who challenge you and ask the tough questions are golden. They'll help you raise your game.

- **People who listen**—They may be hard to find, but these people want to know more about you. They want to help. They ask a lot of questions and listen closely to your answers. These people are a powerful force.

Which groups should you join?

There are countless trade associations and professional clubs. Meetups are hot. Millions of professionals value LinkedIn groups. And, of course, mastermind groups are wildly popular for business owners and professionals who want to gather wisdom and grow.

You might field invitations from friends and colleagues to join groups, and trying them can be time well spent. However, don't let chance decide where you're going to spend your time.

Do some research and aim to select a well-rounded mix of organizations. Asking your peers, influencers, and clients which groups they belong to is a smart approach for targeting worthwhile groups. Of course, the social media activities of your peers will also provide great clues.

Try to diversify your group activities. Any one type won't serve all your needs. Here are several different types of groups to consider:

Mastermind groups

The idea of the "mastermind" group is often attributed to Napoleon Hill's descriptions of the concept in his books, *The Law of Success* and *Think And Grow Rich*. Hill credits Andrew Carnegie for the idea. But Carnegie didn't invent the concept. Historians speak of The Junto, a club established by Benjamin Franklin for the purpose of debating important questions and exchanging knowledge of business affairs.

Masterminds aims to sharpen your business and personal skills to help you achieve success.

- They offer a combination of brainstorming, education, peer accountability, and support in a group setting.
- Participants challenge each other to set and accomplish goals.
- Membership requires commitment, confidentiality, willingness to both give and receive advice and ideas.
- The agenda belongs to the group, and each person's participation is key.

Professional associations

- Professional associations are "knowledge networks" where members tend to be from a specific industry.
- The primary purpose is to exchange information and ideas.
- Members might be potential clients or partners.
- Examples of professional associations: National Association of REALTORS, American Bar Association, American Medical Association, National Speakers Association.

Casual contact business groups

- They accept people from various overlapping professions.
- They usually meet monthly and often hold mixers where members mingle informally.
- Meetings often feature guest speakers or member speakers presenting on business topics.
- Examples include: chambers of commerce, Meetups, networking clubs, events.

Strong contact network groups

- They meet weekly, often for the purpose of exchanging referrals.
- Membership may be restricted to one person per profession or specialty.
- Meetings tend to be more structured, including open networking, short presentations by everyone, and more detailed presentations by one or two members.
- They require a greater commitment from you.
- BNI is an example, with chapters all over the world.

Community service clubs

- These are formed to give back to the community.
- They are good sources of word-of-mouth business.
- Examples include Rotary, Lions and Kiwanis Clubs.

Some other groups

- Company-led communities
- User groups
- Internet-based forums
- Women's groups
- Campus groups
- Church and institutional groups
- And, of course...

Social media groups

Social media groups deserve a special section here because the best engagement online happens in them. People join them for one purpose: to engage with others about a specific topic.

It's sometimes tough to connect with a stranger directly on social media. However, it's easy to spark a conversation with that same person if they're actively involved in one of your groups.

You can find social media groups on any topic under the sun, from aardvarks to zombies. Yes, we verified that. The social media groups you'll want to consider include:

- LinkedIn groups
- Facebook groups
- Google+ groups
- Twitter chats
- Reddit communities

Try not to get sucked into social media groups merely because they get numerous likes and links. Link bombing is not the point. Interaction is. Look for groups where activity levels are high and members are consistently contributing to the comment streams. Real discussions give you a chance to learn, interact and add value. Every post may not generate comments, but if most of them don't you should move on.

Tips for getting started

Join the group
Some groups will allow you to preview discussions in the group before you join. Others will have privacy settings requiring you to join the group first. If you join a group then find out they do not have useful discussions, you can leave the group.

Monitor the discussions
Monitor the discussions and comments for a few days to get a feel for how friendly and responsive its members are.

Search the discussions
If you want to talk about specific topics, try using the search option.

Read the group rules
Every group has unique group rules. Some allow specific kinds of discussions; others don't. Generally, the groups that disallow link sharing and selling are the ones that will have the most meaningful exchanges.

Participate in discussions
Make yourself valuable by replying to posts. Answer questions and chime in with valuable information.

Create insightful posts
Try to be the first to share big news that will interest the members. Start discussions.

Ask questions
Ask questions to engage in interesting conversions.

Get into it

As is the case with so many things, what you get out of groups will be a function of what you put into it. Be a contributor and good citizen. Be generous. Although you join groups to advance your career, you need to remember the group's not all about you.

If you want to build your personal brand, remember to "work" the networking groups you belong to. Connect with the members and make things happen.

There's more to come on networking in—you guessed it— Chapter N.

"**PERSONAL BRANDING, THE WAY I SEE IT, IS REALLY JUST BEING CLEAR ABOUT WHAT YOU DO AND DOING IT WELL. BUT IT'S ALSO TELLING THE STORY IN SUCH A WAY THAT PEOPLE UNDERSTAND WHY TO BOTHER WITH YOU IN THE FIRST PLACE."**

—CHRIS BROGAN

K

is for

Keywords

Position your personal brand with some choice words

Got a personal glossary? When surfers go a-Googling, which words will lead them to you? Build a short list of relevant keywords and use them often on your site and across all your social media profiles.

Keyword research is market research for the 21st century. Knowing that, your personal brand has to take into account what people type into search engines. For example, in my case, I knew that lots of people in the SEO world were searching for keywords like "link building" and "how to get backlinks."

BRIAN DEAN
FOUNDER OF
BACKLINKO

So I initially crafted my personal brand around those topics (and keywords). And it worked! I quickly positioned myself as an expert on those topics. And the rankings soon followed.

K is for Keywords

The Road to Recognition is paved with association. You're not going to be recognized as Kori, Dale, Ashton, or Elvis, for that matter. But you might be recognized as Kori the environmental non-profit leader, Dale the bass guitar expert, Ashton the choreographer, or Elvis the king of rock and roll.

So the question is, "What will people associate with your name?" The answer: a few select words you attach to your brand—keywords.

Whether you search by typing, tapping, or talking, the empty field marked by a little magnifying glass icon is your doorway to discovery. That said, a lot has changed (and continues to change) in search. Google and other popular search engines now interpret your input better than ever. Given all the changes, many observers believe keywords no longer matter. But nothing could be further from the truth.

The search engines of today are insanely powerful. In less than a second, they search billions of indexed pages and return links to those most likely to satisfy your needs—in order of relevance. But as amazing as they are, search engines are unable to read your mind. You have to tell them what you seek. They don't give you anything until you give them some words to work with.

Keep that in mind as you build your personal brand, and plan accordingly. You have to know what you want to be known for.

Think neon

A few years back, the marketing automation leaders at HubSpot wrote, "Keywords are the new neon signs." Awesome. Just as store owners must carefully choose the words they'll display in neon, you'll need to do the same for your brand.

With search technology in mind, you need to carefully consider keyword options and create a shortlist you want to represent your brand. Specificity is all-important.

Dan Schawbel, founder and publisher of the Personal Branding Blog, said it well: "If you want to be known for everything, you'll be known for nothing."

How keywords come into play

Keyword discussions generally go hand in hand with search engine optimization lessons, so we'll start there, but we'll also examine three ways keyword selection comes into play for the personal brander.

Google and web search engines
In Chapter G, we looked at the all-important "Google Yourself" exercise. Because of the ubiquity of search, the results search engines do or don't return when you enter your name are a major reflection of your brand. Now add the idea of expert discovery. You want to associate your brand with keywords that reflect your area of expertise when people search for experts in the niche.

Social media
Chapter L is going to reiterate the crucial relationship between your LinkedIn profile and personal brand. The same keyword selection lesson applies to all the social channels you use—in multiple ways:

The keywords you use in your social profiles enable members of the network to find you via the service's search.

Perhaps even more importantly, they allow the search algorithm of the network to find and suggest your profile and content to fellow members.

Potential followers will scan or speed-read your profile looking for practical reasons to follow you or reach out.

In your own mind
Finally, a search must take place between your ears. You need to define your brand with just a few words—even to the point where you have your own tagline or slogan. The process of selecting keywords will help you think it through.

How to pick your brand's keywords

Keyword selection is the critical first step in SEO. And SEO is such a big and important topic, I could write a book about it. Wait, I already did: *SEO Simplified for Short Attention Spans*. Pick up a copy to unravel the mysteries of search fast. The book offers a variety of ideas for keyword research. Here are some that will help in your pursuits to position yourself with keywords:

- **Think about it**—Brainstorm, baby. You know what you do (or aim to do). There's no better way to begin than simply putting down ideas that come to mind. Don't edit yourself at this point. Let it fly.

- **Job descriptions**—Even if you're not job hunting, try mining job boards for keywords.

- **Competition**—You may or may not consider the established experts in your area your competition, but chances are great you'll find ideas for positioning, and counter-positioning, your brand by examining what your contemporaries do.

- **LinkedIn**—Discover how others use keywords on LinkedIn, particularly in the first line atop their profile.

- **Search tools**—Try these three approaches, courtesy of Google:

  - Note the suggestions you're given as you type in the search field.

  - After completing a search, scroll to the bottom of the page for related keyword phrases.

  - Open a Google AdWords account. Technically, this tool is for planning pay-per-click campaigns, but you don't have to buy a thing to mine Google's deep keyword data with the AdWords Keyword Planner.

  - There are a number of keyword suggestion tools likely to give you ideas beyond what you'll find with Google's tools. Try Ubersuggest and Keywordtool.io.

- **The digital universe**—You can mine keyword ideas from popular web services such as:

- Wikipedia—Most entries are organized in outline form and are rich with phrases related to the topic.

- Udemy—The same goes for Udemy. Check out the course outlines.

- Amazon—Read the reviews. An added bonus of getting keyword ideas from user reviews is you'll discover how your audience actually speaks, writes, and thinks.

- Industry forums—Every niche has loads of online forums where people speak the language of the industry.

Where should you stick these words?

Stick 'em everywhere: everywhere you can, everywhere that makes sense, everywhere your name appears. For starters, work the keywords that represent your personal brand into your:

- **Home page**—Find a place for keywords in the slogan that accompanies your logo or image, on your page's hero image, or in your introduction.

- **About page**—Your keywords are more than a phrase to put on your About page. They're the communications strategy for it.

- **Blog**—As you build your personal brand, your blog will be home to your site's most traveled pages. Position your brand there.

- **Social profiles**—Use your keywords consistently across every social media profile you create.

- **Business cards**—Your business cards and any materials you hand out should include them too.

"You are most proficient at effectively communicating your personal brand when you can describe the interconnected and woven layers that define it in two words or less (your personal brand keywords)."
–Glen Llopis, Forbes contributor (who uses the keywords "opportunity expert" to describe his brand)

is for

LinkedIn

Master the personal branding epicenter of the Internet

Cats and dogs don't belong here. LinkedIn is the social network that means business. It's the personal branding epicenter of the Internet. Take LinkedIn seriously and learn how to work it.

STEPHANIE SAMMONS
AUTHOR OF *LINKEDIN TO INFLUENCE*

LinkedIn is the most powerful business networking resource in history. It is a global, virtual, perpetual networking event!

LinkedIn is currently the best professional platform for growing your personal influence, building a loyal referral network, positioning yourself as a thought leader and attracting your ideal clients.

L is for LinkedIn

LinkedIn enters into every conversation I have about personal branding.

Everything that fuels the ascent of your personal brand lives on LinkedIn. You won't find images or videos about adorable pets there. Unlike other popular social channels, LinkedIn is all business. It's the online center for meeting people, sharing content, and creating and building business relationships.

Even if you enjoy other social media more, LinkedIn must be a part of your media mix. LinkedIn has more than 350 million users from 200+ countries. Forty percent of its members check in daily.

Begin by making your profile professional

Be sure not to rush through the process of creating your LinkedIn profile. More than on any other social media channel, your profile will be visited and read.

Because the personal brand is so central to the LinkedIn environment, you're given a big and flexible canvas on which to paint a picture of yourself. Put some effort, thought, and creativity into rocking your public profile top to bottom.

- **A professional headline**—Below your name, you're given up to 120 characters to populate your headline field. Consider beginning with a tagline to make a first impression. Next, enter a healthy dose of keywords describing yourself and your areas of expertise. You want to be found via relevant searches. Showcase your strengths without being pretentious.

- **Photo**—Your profile is 11X more likely to be viewed if it includes a photo. Your photo should be a high-quality headshot. No points are given for creativity. Look into the lens, make eye contact, and smile.

- **Background**—LinkedIn allows you to upload a background image to serve as your cover photo. Choose an image that reflects well on your brand.

- **URL**—LinkedIn issues you an impossibly long and anonymous URL, but it's easy to customize it with your name, which makes it much easier to remember and share.

- **Summary**—Use the summary section to tell your story as you would on an about page. Include keywords for search purposes, but compose your summary to be warm and informative, aiming to answer basic questions about your skills and inspire visitors to keep reading.

- **Experience**—Populate the fields in the experience section with your work history to present your credentials as you would in a resume.

- **Add media**—In both the experience and education sections, you can display documents, photos, links, presentations, or videos. Using a video will help make your profile stand out.

- **Skills and endorsements**—This section allows you to select your skills and present endorsements given to you from LinkedIn members. Listing your skills gives members a 13X boost in profile views.

- **Recommendations**—Written testimonials are presented here, which are even more powerful than endorsements.

- **Additional information and summary elements**—There's a long list of optional sections you can add to your profile: groups, certifications, publications, projects, honors, organizations, and more. Publish the things you feel are credentials and/or conversation starters and order them as you like.

Building relationships on the network

You shouldn't think of LinkedIn strictly as a place for job hunting. While employment's a big part of the picture, LinkedIn's an ideal place to promote your content, generate leads, find partnership opportunities, and conduct research.

You accomplish all of the above by connecting with LinkedIn members. Let's look at how it's done.

- **Grow your network**—Search the "people you may know" section and you'll find LinkedIn does a great job of populating the list with, you guessed it, people you may know. You can send an automatic invitation with a single click on "connect." If you've imported your email contacts list via "add connections," LinkedIn shows you their email address and the option to send an invitation by clicking "add to network." Additionally, you can run an advanced people search, find alumni, and ask for introductions to the people LinkedIn identifies as second-degree connections.

- **Join groups**—One of the platform's most useful features is LinkedIn Groups, which includes millions of groups catering to all business interests. Groups generally exist to share content and ideas. They also provide another way to identify and make meaningful connections. Use keyword searches to get started finding relevant groups. The results will give you some insights into the group's charter and indicate its size by member count. You also have the option to start your own groups, public or private. Creating a group is a cinch, but understand that managing a group takes a fair amount of time.

Deliver valuable content

In recent years, LinkedIn has expanded to become a giant content marketing hub for individuals and companies.

- **Share your thoughts**—As is the case with all social networks, you need to contribute to the conversation. On your LinkedIn homepage, "share an update" presents a blank field in which you can write your thoughts, upload a photo, and paste a link if you choose.

- **Start a group discussion**—You start discussions within your groups by giving your comment a title and then writing details. Asking questions tends to be the best way to invoke a meaningful discussion.

- **Go one on one**—In the course of your updates and discussions, you're likely to want to engage individually. LinkedIn enables you to do so via LinkedIn email. If you're looking to nurture a "pen pal" relationship into something more, this is how it's done.

- **Publish blog posts**—In 2014, LinkedIn took a bold step toward becoming a content marketing hub by introducing its own publishing platform, which is the easiest blog publishing platform anywhere. It's very intuitive and nice looking too. Publishing a blog post—of any length—on LinkedIn is a wonderful opportunity to reach your ideal audience and support your personal brand.

LinkedIn's loaded with content

SlideShare

In 2012, LinkedIn acquired SlideShare, the world's largest community for sharing presentations, infographics, documents, videos, and PDFs. It's integrated with LinkedIn, making it easy for you to present SlideShare content on your profile page. Use the feature to showcase your portfolio or any type of content that supports your personal brand.

LinkedIn Pulse

LinkedIn Pulse delivers professional news tailored to your interests. It's home to the robust "LinkedINfluencers" blog, which features exclusive posts from hundreds of carefully selected industry leaders across many topics. The news aggregator is available on the LinkedIn site and via smartphone apps.

LinkedIn Premium accounts

You'll do fine developing your personal brand on LinkedIn without investing in paid services; however, you should be aware premium accounts are offered. The premium offering provides a number of value-added services, some of them useful to power users.

LinkedIn analytics

The free analytics provided by LinkedIn to individual members reveal people who have viewed your profile, how you rank among your connections, and some additional insights.

LinkedIn advertising

LinkedIn's advertising options are many. The programs offer powerful B2B targeting features to reach the audience you choose among its nearly 350 million members.

is for

Media

THE ROAD TO RECOGNITION

Channel your energy into the right channels

The web is wide. Media is more complex than ever and more vital. Identify the outlets that are most valued in your field and use the tools available in them to elevate your brand.

JASON MILLER

AUTHOR OF *WELCOME TO THE FUNNEL*

GLOBAL CONTENT MARKETING LEADER AT LINKEDIN

Ever wonder what happened to that personal brand guru who did nothing but focus on Google+? Yeah, they disappeared faster than a one-hit wonder in the 80s. The problem? Putting all of your proverbial eggs in one media basket.

The importance of expanding your personal brand across a variety of social channels and media types cannot be overstated. When it comes to creating content, it's vital that, early on, you have a vision of how that message can be communicated effectively across different platforms through various media. Online, offline, visual, audio, text: how can you deliver your message with maximum potency while re-imagining and repurposing for longevity?

M is for Media

Modern man is a nomadic and erratic channel-hopping media addict.

He or she is multitasking and question-asking. Content consuming. Instant response assuming. He or she is watching, listening, reading, scanning, buffering and planning, snapping, tapping, interacting and reacting. He or she is uploading and downloading, filtering and forwarding, retweeting and deleting, recording and reporting. He or she is changing his or her password, profile picture, privacy preferences, and professional references.

But sometimes he or she chooses just to listen to the radio and chill.

Who knows? The media landscape is nuts. Digital injected an infinity effect, fostered a serve-yourself free-for-all, and made everyone a media enigma to those with a brand promotion agenda.

Your job, should you choose to accept it, is to figure out how to connect with him and her.

Tune into what your audience tunes into

The essence of this chapter is two-fold (and essentially two overlapping ideas). The acceleration of your personal brand relies on identifying:

1. The where: understanding the media channels you need to use to deploy your messaging, and

2. The what: the type of media, or content, you create.

Neither will be cut and dried to the point where the answers fall neatly into place and success comes quickly or easily. Experimentation and analysis will be paramount.

Uncovering the "where" is a critical starting point, especially if you haven't already succeeded in making your website or blog a popular destination (and few have). The end goal is to meet your audience where they spend time. Your first challenge is to figure out where that is and your second is to show up and engage them there.

Analyzing the footprint of your competition and industry influencers is your best starting point. Observe the platforms and channels your competitors are using.

Have leaders in your niche:

- Created strong followings on Facebook, Instagram, Twitter, LinkedIn, Pinterest, YouTube, or SlideShare?

- Succeeded in getting significant engagement (as indicated by shares or comments) via specific digital publishing outlets?

- Established themselves as consistent producers of video or podcasts?

- Leaned heavily on the use of email marketing, search, or digital advertising such as pay-per-click?

- Developed obvious patterns in their use of print, radio, television, mail, or outdoor media?

Some more thoughts:

- Have you ever asked your audience about their media consumption preferences? Try interviews and/or surveys.

- Does the nature of your niche—and maybe its demographics—suggest a substantial leaning toward mobile consumption?

- Can you extract insights from your past efforts about the content that resonated with your audience? You might evaluate which pages get visited most, which assets get downloaded often, and what content invokes shares, comments, and questions.

- Do consumption patterns indicate preferences for certain types of communications over others?

Seth and Barry have both seen differences in their businesses and clients' businesses regarding media tastes, but have found some patterns too. A great example is visual content. Separately and collaboratively, we have produced infographics and SlideShare presentations that have been enormous hits. One such infographic inspired *The Road to Recognition*. In the marketing of this book, we've drawn from the well again with infographics and SlideShare content because we know our audience appreciates them.

Repurpose to increase your reach

Let's concede the answers to the many questions above don't come easily and certainly are not singular. Everyone in your audience doesn't have the same media preferences and most individuals consume a variety of media regularly.

By no means should these realities deter you from researching your audience's media preferences; however, in various forms or fashion, you'll want to cast a net to reach more people with the media they like on the channels they use.

So let's look at a seriously smart media strategy for enhancing and extending your personal branding efforts.

Your content should be repurposed in different forms, enabling you to harness more media with less effort. The idea is to create a hub-and-spoke model with one strong, thematic idea at the center. I'll use an eBook as an example because it will clearly demonstrate the point.

- You strategically develop a multi-chapter eBook addressing a specific but rich topic you can explore deeply.

- Chapters (or variations of them) can be published on your blog and offered to other publications as guest posts. Perhaps some of the content is based on interviews.

- You might make an audio version or repurpose the interviews as podcasts and videos.

- Say the eBook features data culled from industry research. An important list is contained within. As such, you have the makings of at least one infographic and slide show.

- The eBook might have a mini-version, a cheat sheet of some sort. Creating a template or shortcut might be easily done.

- You could present the materials in a webinar or on stage.

- The artwork and interesting quotes from the eBook could fuel your updates across the social media channels you choose.

- You'll certainly want to create email to support the content, maybe even a series of emails or a mini-course.

I could go on but don't need to. You understand. I'm suggesting your content strategy also includes a preconceived media strategy. Your up-front efforts may be larger, but obviously, you wind up getting greater bang for your buck.

Be sure to develop the content with continuity, paying mind to your brand's standards. Take advantage of the "family plan" you've developed by linking your content assets. Cross-reference them whenever you can, and when the content is published in media other than your own, make every attempt to direct the audience to your website and blog. You might also want to create campaign-specific landing pages to capture leads and new subscribers.

Think media-specific

As you develop media for various channels, think specifically about the dynamics of each channel. What would your specific target want from you on Twitter? How might it differ to better support your efforts on LinkedIn? Would you write in a different voice for a white paper? Would your guest post need a new spin for the audience it's presented to?

Your target is a real person accessing your information for different reasons in different media. Keep that in mind. In this fragmented media age, you want to be in many places, but you don't want to be "all over the place." Strive to represent your brand with continuity and maintain its standards.

Take it in stride, execute in steps

From the time I was a kid, media's always fascinated me, and it continues to. The rise of 21st-century digital technologies has sparked a revolution in media.

A good part of my fixation for media traces to my passion for music, which serves as a perfect example. In my (not-so-short) lifetime, music media has evolved to include: radio, MTV, satellite, cable stations, iTunes, podcasts, Spotify, Pandora, Rhapsody, Apple music, Beats, Google Play, Amazon Echo—to name a few.

To say new media has proliferated might be the understatement of this book. Thanks to the Internet, media has been democratized. We can all own a piece of it now and use it as we like. With commitment, strategy, a solid understanding of your audience, and creativity, the potential to build your brand in modern media is limitless.

Given the road we've just traveled in this chapter, I'm now struck with this fear: what if media doesn't fascinate you the way it does me? Perhaps you're intrigued and eager to publish new things, but you're overwhelmed by the unfamiliar territory.

You might have learned Gen Y is all about messaging, commuters consume podcasts, IT geeks download white papers, moms are partial to Pinterest, bloggers read blogs, speakers scan slides, and the C-suite prefers video.

What can you do? If you took it all literally, you'd go out of your media-loving mind. We don't want that. My advice is to take it in stride—and take it in steps. Neither Rome nor Oprah Winfrey's media empire were built in a day.

If you want to accelerate your career with the tactics presented in this book, you do need to warm up to new media, but it'd be reckless to "floor it." Rather than trying to race your way to a litany of media types and channels, simply devise a way to shift to the next gear. Select a media play that makes sense for your brand and roll with it.

"YOUR PERSONAL BRAND SERVES AS YOUR BEST PROTECTION AGAINST BUSINESS FACTORS YOU CAN'T CONTROL."

—DAN SCHAWBEL

is for

Network

THE ROAD TO RECOGNITION

Connect with professionals— and with purpose

Make friends. Make connections fearlessly and frequently—locally, regionally, and globally. Have a business card or something of even greater value to distribute. Follow up and follow through.

SCOTT ABEL
FOUNDER OF THE
CONTENT WRANGLER

Your audience is your most powerful asset. Include them in your successes—and share your ideas, knowledge, experience, and connections with them. But don't stop there. Ask your audience for help when you feel defeated or could use a little extra creative juice.

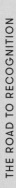

Developing a network and sense of camaraderie amongst your peers reduces competitive friction and enables you to borrow the power of the crowd to extend the reach of your brand. When you connect and engage with your audience, everyone feels like part of something bigger. Your network of friends and associates can be your biggest brand evangelists.

N is for Network

network, noun—a group of interconnected people who work with each other. You need to have this.

network, verb—to talk to people for business opportunities or advice. You need to do this.

networking, noun—the exchange of information or services among individuals, groups, or institutions; the cultivation of productive relationships for employment or business.

Networking is essential for building your personal brand and will prove key to achieving your goals. Networking not only opens doors to new opportunities but also helps you create lasting relationships to build on. You never know where or when you'll meet your next boss, client, partner, employee, investor, or the person who'll connect you to someone with the ideal sphere of influence.

Well-connected people have influence. Their power is based on the social capital they've earned by building relationships with those in their network. You don't build social capital with people by "friending" or following them. There's no question you should use social networks to expand and accelerate your efforts; however, to create truly meaningful relationships, you need to cultivate them offline.

Networking's work

Networking's not free. You'll have to invest time and money into building your network and "working it." Will it be worth it? Let's take a look at the potential benefits (you read about some of them in Chapter J).

- **Referrals**—Referrals are serious door openers and will foster a much higher trust factor.

- **Opportunities**—Opportunities might include joint ventures, client leads, partnerships, speaking, writing opportunities, and more.

- **Visibility**—You raise your profile with increased visibility and opportunities to build your reputation. The more you show up, the more likely you are to benefit.

- **Advice**—Through your network, you gain the opportunity to get valuable advice and expertise.

- **Positive influence**—Those you hang out with and talk to influence your outlook. Surrounding yourself with positive, uplifting people will help you thrive.

- **Confidence**—Networking can be a confidence booster because it pushes you to sharpen your social skills, grow, and learn.

- **Satisfaction**—A common theme in this book is "givers get." You'll find it satisfying and rewarding to help people in your network solve problems and make progress.

- **Friendships**—You'll form friendships and have fun.

Get ready to network

Many of the personal branding tools and techniques we've covered in *The Road to Recognition* should help prepare you for success at networking events or when cultivating relationships in any setting. Essential tools that will help you prepare effectively include:

- **Business card**—Whether you're employed or not, have a nicely designed business card handy to give to networking contacts. The card should include your contact information and some expression of your brand (logo, tagline, etc.). Include your website/blog URL, and possibly key social network IDs as well. Many personal branders choose to include a photo, which can help people remember you later.

- **Resume**—Create a polished resume. Get help, if needed. Unless you're job hunting, you probably won't be handing out resumes at events, but for most professionals, it's wise to have an up-to-date resume ready when needed.

- **Social media profiles**—We covered this topic in the LinkedIn chapter, so I'll be brief. Have well-written, keyword-optimized, descriptive profiles published and current across all the social networks you use.

- **Elevator pitch**—Your "elevator pitch" is a 30 to 60 second introduction to your personal brand. You want to be able to quickly articulate your unique qualities, abilities, and interests. It's smart to practice your elevator pitch. You might test it on trusted colleagues or record yourself delivering it. The most common way you'll deliver your elevator pitch will be when meeting someone for the first time and answering a question such as "What brings you here?" or "What do you do?" or "Can you tell me about yourself?" After delivering your pitch, keep the conversion going and switch quickly into "good listener" mode by asking your new acquaintance an open-ended question.

- **Your smart phone**—A smart approach: have your smart phone on hand. You might want to take photos, share something of value, or make an immediate connection on LinkedIn or another relevant group or network.

- **Grab bag**—A little creativity (and possibly investment) goes a long way toward making a memorable first impression. You can one-up the standard business card exchange with a small gift. Some ideas I've employed (or seen used) include:
  - Magnet
  - Bookmark
  - Pen
  - Notebook
  - Brochure
  - T-shirt

You can make a very powerful impression by handing out a book. If you've written a book, consider handing out copies. It's also possible to give the people you meet a book you recommend, were quoted in, or have some connection to.

For practical purposes, in most settings you'll need to rely on your case or backpack to tote your swag collection around, so most of the ideas I've presented are small and lightweight.

A t-shirt, book, or something bigger and perhaps more expensive isn't necessary. It's the thought that counts, right?

But consider this powerful networking tip: follow up after the event by delivering a physical present or package of some sort. You can imagine what a powerful impression you'll make with this approach.

On a few occasions, I've come home from a conference to find a package waiting for me. That's thoughtful networking.

Whatever you do or say at a networking event, do what you say you're going to do (and maybe more). Follow up. Every time. With everyone. If you said you'd call, connect online, or send something, make absolutely sure you do it. Many don't, which is an opportunity wasted and obviously detrimental to the trust-building mission you're on.

Of course, to follow up consistently, you need to remember every promise you made, so create a way to record them. Your phone might come in handy. I tend to jot notes on the back of the person's business card.

Your advanced planning for a networking event might also include preparing to speak to specific people you expect to be there. Will there be speakers, panelists, or special guests you'd like to meet for the first time? If so, do some research on them. If they're an author, you might buy their book before or at the event. You could listen to their podcasts, watch their videos, or read their blogs. It's easier to start a conversation when you know something about the people you approach—and they'll appreciate it too.

Go forth and meet people

You already have a network of some sort. It may be modest and you may not be taking advantage of it. If so, it's time to make a conscious effort to expand your network and establish beneficial relationships.

Understand networking etiquette. Here are some action items and tips you'll want to consider putting into play.

- **Give yourself some goals**—You might set a goal to have one or more networking calls each week. You could set goals for X number of new referrals too. Put time on your calendar to devote specifically to networking.

- **Get involved**—As we talked about in chapter J, join relevant organizations.

- **Examine your current network**—Think through the current connections you have, including friends, family, teachers, peers, and people within organizations you belong to. Include those you've come to know via social media. Make a list and organize your contacts with a Rolodex or contact database. Reconnect. Reach out and ask for recommendations and referrals.

- **Go all-in on LinkedIn**—Just a reminder here to heed the advice in chapter L.

- **Do interviews**—Create content and network at the same time by asking to do interviews with influencers in your niche.

- **Attend conferences**—Professional conferences and events are where you'll find the movers and shakers and most active networkers. Make a point to attend at least one per year, more if your budget allows. Go prepared to meet the stars of the show.

- **Work the event**—Recognize that everyone at industry events also wants to network. Don't monopolize any one person's time. Aim to spend five to ten minutes with each person. End the conversation politely and consider discussing how you'll follow up or keep in touch.

- **Make a good impression**—Make your first-time encounters count. Make eye contact with the person you're talking to and stay focused on him or her. You want to show the person you're sincerely interested, so avoid scanning the room and planning your next introduction. Ask thoughtful questions.

- **Avoid selling**—Forget about selling and focus only on relationship building. Ask the people you meet how you can help them.

"PERSONAL BRANDING IS NOT AS EASY AS FILLING IN THE BLANKS. IF YOU TRULY WANT TO STAND OUT, YOU WILL HAVE TO BE AWARE OF YOUR ENVIRONMENT AND THINK CRITICALLY ABOUT WHAT ASSETS YOU HAVE AND HOW TO LEVERAGE THEM TO YOUR ADVANTAGE. YOUR BRAND IS ARGUABLY YOUR MOST IMPORTANT ASSET. ISN'T IT WORTH INVESTING IN?"

—KAREN KANG

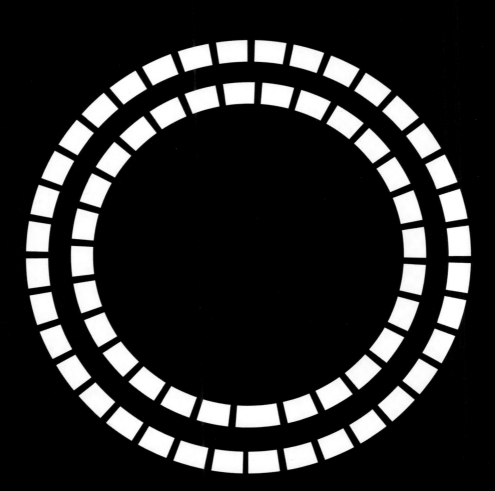

is for **Offers**

Offer your visitors great value—for free

Meet readers where they're @. Expand your email list, build relationships, and position yourself as an authority by offering your readers value-added content—or lead magnets—in exchange for an email address.

CHRIS SMITH

AUTHOR OF *THE CONVERSION CODE*

CO-FOUNDER OF CURAYTOR

Social media is a great way to connect to your audience, but email is even better. So if you're doing the hard work of building your personal brand through online channels, focus on building an email list.

The key is creating great content and presenting it as irresistible "offers" for your readers. Get in that mindset and get good at developing great offers. You'll be rewarded with subscribers and have the opportunity to use the all-important email channel to build relationships, and of course, your personal brand.

O is for Offers

Good news. I just received several emails alerting me that visitors to my site subscribed to my email list. It happens every day, but it's not because I ask readers to "sign up for my newsletter." It's because I offered them something of value.

Personal branders are givers. You've got that by now. But of course, this book is about accelerating your professional success. You want to get things, yet here we are again talking about giving.

It's called reciprocity—a powerful principle of influence—and a simple slice of human psychology. When someone does something for you, you feel obliged to give back. In the spirit of reciprocity, we'll now dive into a chapter about gift giving. The ideas will focus on making valuable offers via a web page to help you:

- Build your email list (or capture any contact information)
- Build relationships
- Gain recognition as a subject matter expert

Choose a magnetic topic

The pulling power of your offer requires a firm handle on what your audience wants information and advice about. The good news is the online behavior of your audience will help provide the direction you need.

- **Search**—Mine the free Google AdWords Keyword Planner to determine search volume for keyword phrases and to review related suggestions.

- **Social shares**—Use Buzzsumo to search by topics and gather insights regarding social shares. Use that intel to isolate trending topics that would make perfect lead magnets.

- **Analytics**—If you've been creating content for any period of time, your Google Analytics will reveal the content your readers find interesting.

- **Q&A sites**—Spend some time on Q&A sites such as Quora and Yahoo! Answers. Similarly, check out forums and groups in your niche.

- **Reviews**—Mining user reviews is an amazing (and underutilized) way to get inside your prospects' minds. Read the reviews at mega content sites such as Amazon, Udemy, and iTunes to gather real-world insights about what turns your people on.

Create a great freebie

So you landed on a good idea. Now make a great lead magnet.

- **Be specific**—Tell your audience exactly what they're going to get. There's nothing compelling about a vague offer. Be ultra-clear about the benefit of opting in for your free content.

- **Deliver a desired result**—Capture the attention of your prospects with a lead magnet promising to move them closer to a desired result.

- **Provide instant gratification**—Everyone wants shortcuts, the fast track, lessons they can apply immediately.

- **Be the authority**—Demonstrate you're the expert. A great lead magnet advances relationships by increasing trust. Create it with the goal of proving you're the best person to help with the problem.

- **Make it worth money**—Free or not, the content you create that will help you realize your branding goals should be valuable to the point where people would pay for it if asked.

- **Make it look great**—Don't compromise on presentation. Invest the time or money needed to create a handsome design.

20 ideas for your offer

Here's a list of strong contenders for your first (or next) offer:

- eBook
- White paper
- Video or video series
- Webinar
- Research report
- Tip sheet
- Checklist
- Resource guide
- Template
- Assessment
- Digital tool
- Mini-course
- Presentation
- Membership
- Infographic or poster
- Calendar
- Demonstration
- Product trial
- Consultation
- Coupon

Effective list building tactics

You have a lead magnet, but it doesn't sell itself, so in this section, we'll look at effective ways to showcase your offer and succeed with your email list building efforts.

- **Landing page**—One of the most effective ways to capture email leads is through a landing page, which showcases your free resource. For optimum conversion, your landing pages should have a singular focus and not include navigational elements that could act as an escape route for the reader.

- **Pop-up forms**—Pop-ups have become popular and less repulsive to users in recent years. They're offered in a variety of forms (light box, slide-ins, scroll-induced, exit-induced, etc.) with various features. Don't knock 'em. They work.

- **Feature box or banner**—A less intrusive alternative to the pop-up is the feature box. It's basically a row on your website—generally on the home page—which functions like a pop-up, but is a permanent fixture.

- **Preview page**—Another approach gaining momentum is the homepage preview (or "take-over") page. That is, when a new visitor arrives, the first thing loaded is an offer-based landing page of sorts that dominates the page.

- **Membership page**—This strategy is sometimes referred to as "hub page" or "resource page." The idea is to create a valuable collection of content on a specific topic, promote it centrally via a single page, and make it available exclusively to those who opt into a free membership.

- **Sidebar**—Placing a form in the sidebar of your homepage, blog, or anywhere across your website is a popular convention and is made easy by your email service provider.

- **Call-to-action (CTA) box**—You may want to create a CTA box to be placed strategically on select pages that do not include a form. A click directs readers to a page where they can opt in.

- **Video**—You can actually generate opt-ins with your video marketing. Create a free, ungated video and insert an offer within it at the halfway point or end. YouTube allows you to create in-video links, as do online video platforms.

- **Content upgrade**—A content upgrade is meant to capture an email address from a blog reader. Somewhere in your post, you offer an additional free asset, usually a PDF.

- **Guest posts**—When you publish a guest post on a blog, offer a lead magnet by including a link to it in your author bio.

- **Social media**—Mention or feature your lead magnet on your profile page, in your cover photo, or in updates. Of course, you can also run ads via most social media channels.

- **Webinar**—Offer webinars related to your offer or mention them as a bonus for registering.

- **Speaking engagement**—When you speak or participate in a panel, be sure the audience is aware you have a free and valuable bonus for them.

"YOU ARE 100% RESPONSIBLE FOR THE IMPRESSION PEOPLE HAVE OF YOU."
—JILL ROWLEY

is for

Podcast

Turn on a mic and say what's on your mind

Get people to listen to you. Top professionals appear on podcasts and create their own shows to capitalize on the format's growing popularity and because they understand the power voice offers for making genuine connections.

JOHN LEE DUMAS

AUTHOR OF *THE FREEDOM JOURNAL*

HOST OF EOFIRE

Podcasting is a special medium of communication. The podcast host and the listener form an intimate connection due to the nature of the audio-only format. This makes podcasting an important part of your brand development because every word you speak is creating know/like/trust with your audience. Once you have established know/like/trust, simply ask what your listeners are struggling with, listen to their pain points, and provide the solution.

Podcasting will open the door to your audience, and I suggest you walk right in.

P is for Podcast

Personal branding is not only about finding your voice but making it heard.

Podcasting represents another exciting example of the democratization of media and an amazing opportunity to be heard. Anyone can create a podcast without the need to make significant financial investments.

You simply invest your time in building your audience, and then seek to find listeners who'll return the favor. Once you do, a certain kind of media magic happens. Podcasts have the power to educate, entertain, inform, inspire, get laughs, incite tears, and touch listeners on an emotional level.

Because few things are more personal than the sound of the human voice, podcasting presents a unique opportunity to connect with your audience. The impression can be even stronger than with content you write.

Podcasts are on the rise too. The medium has grown steadily the past three years: 21 percent of Americans now listen to podcasts, mostly with mobile devices and, often, with impressive loyalty. Edison Research says the same number of Americans listen to podcasts as are active on Twitter.

The Road to Recognition covers a gamut of content formats, but podcasting stands out as the ultimate blend of intimacy and ease. Podcasts can be consumed comfortably and safely while multitasking, which helps explain the popularity and steady growth of the medium.

The medium is uniquely convenient and portable. In transit, in the gym, on a dog walk, anywhere, anytime, podcast subscribers invite audio content into their ears. "You don't have to plan your life around podcasts. You plan podcasts around your life," wrote Copyblogger's Jerod Morris.

So now hear this: podcasting is perfect for personal branding.

Be a good guest

Your getting-started plan for podcasting could simply be to focus first on becoming a featured guest on existing programs. To land interview spots, you need to get on the radar of podcast hosts and give them a reason to have you on their show. It's easier than you might imagine. My recommendations:

- **Get to know the playing field**—Identify the popular shows in your niche via search and podcast outlets such as iTunes, Stitcher, and SoundCloud. Take the time to listen to the podcasts you've identified.

- **Identify your primary targets**—Narrow the list to under 20 interview-style shows that do guest interviews and find the right person to contact via the host's website.

- **Write effective outreach email**—You need to proactively answer the question, "Why would I be a great guest?" by effectively communicating the value you'll bring to the program's audience. An effective template for this type of pitch email might include:

  - A brief and friendly introduction

  - The topics for which you could deliver great value

  - A short bio, including where you may have been featured in the past

  - Information about your current audience (if possible)

  - Testimonials and/or accolades

  - Links to examples of your content

  - A mention that you have quality recording equipment

- **Always follow up**—Remember, you're building a network, so follow up whether you're accepted or not. Your time may come.

- **Prepare to be the best guest ever**—Give each interview your all, whether the show's audience is big or small. Research the host, listen to his or her shows, note questions the host likes to ask, and practice your responses.

- **Promote your guest appearances**—Part of being a good guest is helping to spread the word. Make your audience aware of your podcast interviews and leverage them in future pitches.

Create your own show

Of course, you don't need to wait until you've become a popular guest interviewee to begin your podcasting journey. It's neither expensive nor difficult to create your own show. Any office will suffice as a studio, and your needs otherwise are modest:

- **Quality microphone**—Listeners will forgive unpolished performances but not sub-par sound. Invest in a USB microphone to assure audio quality.

- **Headphones**—Even ear pods will do.

- **Microphone stand**—Mount the mic to your desk with a boom or simply bring it to the level of your mouth with a desktop stand.

- **A place to record**—Use a quiet room, preferably a small space that doesn't create a hollow sound.

- **Editing software**—Many applications, including Garage Band, Adobe Audition, Camtasia, and Audacity (free) will give you the tools you need to edit audio.

Podcast formats differ, so you'll want to pick a show format that suits you.

- **Interviews**—The popular interview format allows you to leverage influencers to help build your audience. (Seth hosts *The Craft of Marketing* with this format.)

- **Multi-host**—The multi-host format is a platform for two or more hosts to converse. (Barry and Andy Crestodina co-host *Content Matters* with this format.)

- **Solo**—Your program can be just you delivering news, opinions, tutorials, or any content.

- **Narrative**—Narrative podcasts are story-driven shows that rely on heavy editing to splice together a cohesive story, pulling from interviews, sound bites, sound effects, and music.

- **Video**—While we cover video in detail in chapter V, note that video podcasts make it easy to create multiple content assets with each episode.

Your guide to getting started

The best podcasts are carefully planned. We'll look at planning considerations now, Q&A style.

- **Are you ready?** As the host, you should be in control of the show and have a good command of how it will unfold. Research topics and guests in advance to podcast like a pro.

- **Do you need scripts?** Some formats are prescripted to some degree, but for most shows, it should suffice to go into recording with an outline, agenda, and/or list of topics or questions.

- **How long should your episodes be?** Interview shows tend to run 20 to 60 minutes. Other formats lend themselves to shorter episodes. You'll want to take into account the production requirements and consider audience preferences.

- **When will your shows go online?** The listen-when-you-want aspect of podcasting makes scheduling less stringent than traditional broadcasting. However, delivering new shows on a consistent schedule will help you set expectations and build an audience.

- **Do you need intros and outros?** Prerecorded introductions and "outros" often feature music, sound effects, and narration. They're not necessary but add a professional touch.

- **Should a podcast have a call to action?** It's more useful to suggest listeners take some action than to simply say goodbye at the conclusion of your show. You might ask listeners to write a review, share, download something, visit a webpage, or buy from a sponsor. You could also talk about the episode on deck, which might actually inspire a listener to tune in again or continue listening right then and there.

- **Where does the show go?** You need to select a podcast hosting platform. SoundCloud and Libsyn are the two most popular podcast hosting services. These and others will make it easy for you to syndicate your show to the major podcast outlets such as iTunes, Stitcher, and podcast apps.

- **What about your website and blog?** Your podcast should have a home on your website where you embed your audio files. You may want to publish transcriptions or detailed posts. Most hosts create abbreviated show notes listing highlights, which help search engines discover your content and give readers incentives to listen.

How to promote your podcast

It's not easy to make your podcast (or any content) stand out in the crowd, but it should be a goal. Dedicate yourself to making it special. Find authoritative guests, develop unique angles, and ask interesting questions. Promote your podcast as the one that delivers a special blend of information and entertainment.

Unsurprisingly, in a book dedicated to branding, I want to stress the power of branding with a number of suggestions.

- **Give the show a catchy name**—Make it short and sweet so it's memorable and legible when included on your cover art.

- **Design great cover art**—A 1400-pixels square image is standard. It will be used as the thumbnail for your show on podcast player apps and is the cover by which you'll be judged by potential new listeners.

- **Make a beautiful landing page**—Create a well-designed landing page where people can learn more about you and the show.

- **Optimize for search**—Use relevant keywords in your show's profile pages, in the titles and descriptions of the episodes, and on the pages they are presented.

Promote your podcast on an ongoing basis with these tactics:

- **Get testimonials**—Social proof in the form of testimonials and reviews will help you market the show. Unfortunately they don't always come easily. Ask your friends, guests, and influencers to write reviews for you.

- **Promote each episode**—Get the word out for each and every episode via social media and other channels, including advertising, if your budget allows.

- **Send your guests email**—If you have guests or mention individuals or companies on your show, send them an email when the episode goes live asking them to share it with their audience.

- **Send email updates**—Alert your email subscribers every time a new episode goes online.

- **Network with other podcasters**—One of the best ways to promote your podcast is getting the attention of established podcasters. Follow the top podcasts in your niche and interact with the hosts. Help promote them and they may return the favor.

Your podcast isn't likely to be a huge hit right away. It can take months or years to build a loyal audience. Stick with it. And keep in mind, even without a large audience, podcasting produces opportunities and personal branding benefits in a variety of ways.

Q is for Questions

Ask your audience to join the conversation

Everyone loves a good listener. Identify the questions your audience seeks answers to. Ask questions. Ask people to tell you their stories. Ask for their ideas. And listen closely.

IAN ALTMAN
AUTHOR OF *SAME SIDE SELLING*

No matter how compelling your facts or how passionately you argue your points, you will never make a statement that is more compelling to influence others than by asking great questions. Yet, not all questions are created equally. You've heard leading questions that attorneys ask: "Isn't it true that…?" You've heard salespeople ask questions like, "What will it take me to get you into this car today?" Each of those questions has a manipulative tone with a not-so-hidden ulterior motive.

The most compelling questions merely seek to discover the truth. Ask your client a question like, "What happens if you don't solve this issue?" Instead of wondering what alternatives they have considered, you could ask, "What else have you tried in seeking a solution?" Honest, open questions set the tone for an even-handed, same-side discussion. If you really want to build trust, you can even ask, "Is this issue worth spending the money to address? Why?"

Whereas devious questions might repel interest, the right questions instill confidence, build trust, and stimulate discovery. You've certainly been inspired by great questions in your life, haven't you?

Q is for Questions

When you were a preschooler, you asked a zillion questions. In the years since, you've probably been broken of the habit. All too often, in school and in business, our focus turns to delivering answers.

Personal branding calls for asking questions of yourself and those you hope to influence. Game-changing ideas come from asking questions. It can shift the way you think about something and open up new possibilities. Asking insightful questions earns you greater trust and respect from those you work with. It's a first step in solving problems and makes you a more successful leader.

This chapter focuses on harnessing the power of questions.

How do questions beget solutions?

Creative problem solving begins with asking questions. In researching ideas for this chapter, I came across the "SCAMPER" technique, an acronym to inspire you to look at different ways of taking on challenges and triggering new ideas. Here's what each letter means and examples of how you might apply the exercise:

- **S (Substitute)**: What can I substitute in my brand development process?

- **C (Combine)**: How can I combine personal branding with other activities?

- **A (Adapt)**: What can I adapt from someone else's approach?

- **M (Magnify)**: What can I magnify to accelerate my success?

- **P (Put to Other Uses)**: How can I put my branding effort to other uses?

- **E (Eliminate)**: What can I eliminate or simplify?

- **R (Rearrange)**: How can I change or rearrange the way I'm doing things?

A great thing about posing questions to yourself is your brain automatically and immediately starts working on them and will keep working on them in the background.

Another effective technique, which I use often when trying to help clients develop marketing messages, is asking why. Often, I'll ask it multiple times in a row. It works wonders for getting to the core of the problem and, therefore, closer to the solution.

Framing a problem as a question helps boost your effectiveness as a problem-solver. Why? Statements trigger our logical and analytical skills and encourage you to try to reach conclusions quickly, while questions trigger our imagination and creative thinking skills. They encourage you explore more, which may foster new insights.

What kinds of questions do leaders ask?

Leaders ask questions to guide and direct critical thinking. Open-ended questions are especially powerful for eliciting new ideas, gathering opinions, and expanding possibilities. For example, "What are your thoughts on this idea?" or "Can you think of some other ways to approach this challenge?"

"Closed" questions are helpful too. These types of questions help direct thinking and sharpen the focus on solutions. For example, "What tasks will get this done most effectively?"

Leaders rely on questions to teach and coach because they recognize it accelerates learning. When leaders ask questions in business environments, they not only guide people to think for themselves but encourage a sense of pride and ownership in the solutions generated.

What makes a question asker so engaging?

The answer is empathy. In branding, marketing, sales, and anywhere you might aim to win people over, empathy is all-important. Listening is the key to creating conversations, developing an understanding of how to be more useful, and ultimately, building relationships.

Ever notice or been in a conversation that is really two simultaneous monologues? Neither person is listening but, rather, waiting his turn to talk (or interrupting). This, of course, is the antithesis of good conversation. Only by making people feel included and listened to can you engage in meaningful and productive conversation.

Make people know you're listening by asking questions about what they said. Want to get serious about this? When you have a follow-up conversation, ask questions about what you learned in the previous conversation. I'm always impressed when people inquire again about something we've talked about prior. They're often looking for the "exit" report. For example, "How'd that conference go for you?" She remembered! Cool. She honestly cares about me.

Do you know where to find good questions?

They are all over the Internet. You could make a case that the Internet is basically a web of questions and answers. This is certainly a viable point of view for approaching search and social media and, therefore, the development of your content.

Obviously, a recurring theme of *The Road to Recognition* is increasing your visibility and authority by delivering value with the things you write, say, share, and present. You can get good at this really fast by delivering insightful answers to your audience's pressing questions. How do you know what they are? You listen, of course. I'm glad you beat me to the answer ;-)

It's easy to listen online

There's no doubt that offering your ideas via social media can be a big part of your personal branding endeavors. However, the potential to extract ideas from social media might be even more powerful.

Again, social media is the greatest market research tool ever. The free-form nature of social media sets ideas free. The conversation is often perfectly candid—organic, you might say.

I don't believe this was the case with many old-school market research techniques. Focus groups, for example, put people on the spot and inspire contrived responses. Surveys, though helpful, tend to rely on multiple-choice questionnaires, which can make the answers forced. Often, the market research of yesteryear was tainted merely by the way the sample was selected or incentivized to participate.

Make social media your market research vehicle, and you can be an entirely inconspicuous fly on the wall. You just read, view, watch, and listen.

You can ask questions, but sometimes all you need to do is simply identify them. They are everywhere:

- Use keywords searches (the use of hashtags often helps) on most social channels to find conversations and questions about anything.
- Search Q&A sites, including Quora, Yahoo! Answers, and Answers.com.
- Find Q&A sites dedicated to your industry. Check StackExchange, a massive network of Q&A communities.
- Read forums in your niche. Find them by searching "niche" and (+forum). There are forums for every conceivable topic and they overflow with questions.

Are you questioning your actions?

Our hope is this book will plant all kind of helpful questions in your mind about your career. Asking questions for self-reflection and goal setting are all-important. It'll help you solve problems, explore opportunities, adapt and adjust, and simply get things done.

"What if..." is amongst the most powerful questions you can ask. The question has the power to direct your imagination,

"YOU HAVE TO HAVE A BRAND TO BE RELEVANT TODAY. THE WORLD HAS CHANGED. ANYONE WITH A SMARTPHONE IS NOW A JOURNALIST. YOU HAVE COMPUTERS WRITING ARTICLES. HOW ARE YOU AND I GOING TO STAY RELEVANT TODAY? HOW IS ANYONE GOING TO STAY RELEVANT TODAY? IT'S YOUR BRAND."

—MARK W. SCHAEFER

create a vision, and inform your plan. The exercise can continue:

- What do I love most?

- What am I doing when I'm at my best?

- What do I want to be known for?

- Am I on the right path?

- How can I improve?

- Am I pushing myself?

- Am I learning?

- Do I have the confidence to achieve my goal?

Feeling inspired? Questioning is the ultimate tool to stimulate thinking. Make it a habit and cultivate it. Asking the right questions to the right people—including yourself—will help power your journey down *The Road to Recognition*. But remember, asking effective questions is a skill. Like any skill, mastering it takes practice.

is for

Recognizing Others

Point to the people who empower you

Share the spotlight. You won't achieve your goals on your own. Privately and publicly, recognize the contributions of every person who's played a part in your brand development.

The secret to building your personal brand is in how you recognize others. Connections with colleagues, influencers, and industry thought leaders are essential to building your personal brand. Engage with them by featuring their best attributes at convention mixers and participating in the conversations they're having on social media.

BRYAN KRAMER
AUTHOR OF *SHAREOLOGY*
CEO OF PUREMATTER

Remember that relationships serve as the cornerstone of every business deal. So using your circle of influence to help others is the very best thing you can do to contribute in a mutually beneficial relationship.

R is for Recognizing Others

This book focuses on building your personal brand and earning recognition. You can't do it alone. And you won't succeed if you focus only on yourself. You need to understand—and recognize—the value other people bring to your career and life.

Who are they? They're the people who inspire you—those whose content you learn from and reach out to for advice. They're also the people you inspire—those who learn from your content and turn to you for advice.

Get in the habit of recognizing friends and colleagues and your efforts won't go unnoticed. Recognition tends to be reciprocal.

Elevating your brand

In his book, *Launch*, author Michael Stelzner, founder of Social Media Examiner, offers what he calls "The Elevation Principle."

Great content + other people - marketing messages = growth.

Stelzner says great content, such as how to articles and success stories, is the fuel of your brand. Other people refers to knowledgeable experts you can bring to your community—speakers, authors, and influential bloggers.

You've probably noticed, I'm using another expert to deliver this lesson. By now, you've also noticed *The Road to Recognition* is crammed full of insights from experts.

Collaborating on content is a powerful way to recognize your influencers, peers, friends, and followers. If, for some reason, you skipped forward to this chapter before reading "I is for Influencers," go back and check it out for a list of ideas.

Make every day Thanksgiving

Gratitude is a powerful message. As you develop your personal brand, you're going to have plenty of reasons to be thankful to your connected network of friends. You may find yourself getting:

- New followers on social media
- Social shares
- Comments from readers
- Positive reviews and endorsements
- Write-ups in blogs and publications
- Mentions in speeches, webinars, and presentations
- Inclusions in roundups
- Invitations to be interviewed
- Business referrals

Reciprocate. Recognize the people who went out of their way to recognize you. Let them know you appreciate them in the following ways:

- Share their content.
- Contribute comments to their blogs and social media streams.
- Endorse them on LinkedIn.
- Write recommendations for them on LinkedIn or testimonials for their websites.
- Send thank you notes or modest gifts via snail mail.
- Write reviews of their books or other written and recorded content they have published.
- Introduce them to editors, collaborators, event coordinators, etc.
- Refer them to appropriate prospects.
- Offer to contribute to their blogs, podcasts, or other content types.
- Invite them to collaborate with you on content.

Small or big, online or off, however you recognize the people who have played some part in fueling the development of your personal brand, it is a meaningful gesture that won't go unnoticed. The important thing is simply to do it.

Be thankful. Be genuine. Find ways to show your appreciation daily.

Andy Crestodina, our friend and the strategic director of Orbit Media, was a big help with this chapter with his post, *15 Ways to Say Thank You to Your Network*. Thank you, Andy, for those words of wisdom—and all you do.

Thank you, too, to everybody who contributed to *The Road to Recognition*.

"ONE OF THE EASIEST AND MOST PRODUCTIVE WAYS TO POSITION YOURSELF AS AN INDUSTRY LEADER, A TRENDSETTER, OR AN EXPERT IS TO SPEAK AT CONFERENCES, TRADE SHOWS, AND EVENTS. IT'S ALSO ONE OF THE SMARTEST WAYS TO TURN ONLINE PERSONAL BRANDS INTO AN OFFLINE POWERHOUSE."

—ANDREW DAVIS

is for

Speaking

Get in front of an audience

The power of the podium is undeniable.
Public speakers gain credibility as
subject matter experts and enjoy
many networking benefits. You
need to step up to the mic and
share what you know.

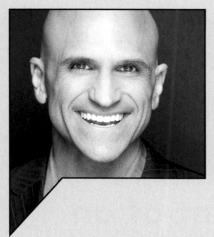

MICHAEL PORT
AUTHOR OF *STEAL THE SHOW*
FOUNDER OF HEROIC PUBLIC SPEAKING

Perhaps you have a speech to deliver at an industry conference. Maybe you're attempting to land a big project. You could be preparing for a job interview that will make or break your career.

Public speaking plays a critical role in building

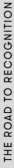

your brand because people expect you to be able to perform in all contexts, including online.

And, when I say perform, I don't just mean that you will do something or complete something. I mean you will present, act, stage, show, or dramatize. You'll put on a performance that delights, impresses, wows, connects, or moves people to think, feel, or do something different.

S is for Speaking

The power of public speaking is undeniable. The person at the front of the room delivering a speech is perceived as an authority. Perfect, but...

Many people would rather be covered by spiders than speak in public. It's time to get past this fear (of speaking, not spiders).

The Visible Expert, a great book from Hinge Marketing, a leading branding and marketing firm for professional services, studies the tactics employed by "visible experts," which they define as professionals who have attained high visibility in the marketplace and a reputation for expertise. The authors claim, "When asked which factors were most important to career development, visible experts put speaking and writing ability at the top of the list, second only to passion and enthusiasm."

Clearly, those that want to fast-track their careers put an emphasis on speaking. Landing speaking opportunities is one of the best ways to boost your personal brand. Public speaking is a highly effective way to:

- Show people who you are and put a face to your brand.
- Introduce you to new people and open doors to new networks.
- Get your message out and showcase the value you deliver.
- Generate publicity.
- Develop your knowledge and persuasion skills.

Are you freaking out now? Take a deep breath. Let's agree overcoming the fear of public speaking is do-able, desirable, and a downright smart thing to do. You can do it.

Say it: "I'm a speaker"

Like anything you want to become, you begin by making the statement. Then what? Here's an action plan to break into public speaking and continue earning greater opportunities.

Develop potential topics

You'll need to think through the topics you can speak about, create a small portfolio of titles and blurbs to describe them, and highlight their value. You can proceed to develop outlines and slides (if you'll use them) or do so after you're booked for a talk.

You may want to test topics by developing them first as written works or delivering them via a webinar. You could also offer to deliver your talk live to one person or a small audience and gather feedback immediately after.

Take what you can get

The big gigs you'll aim for in the future aren't likely to fall into your lap right away. However, speakers are always needed, so be prepared to accept small gigs and speak for free.

You might volunteer to speak to professional and industry associations, nonprofit organizations, colleges, chambers of commerce, etc. You'll gain experience and the practice will do you good. Hopefully, you'll collect some testimonials and referrals. Paid speaking gigs and bigger opportunities will come in time.

Scope your future

Create a list of potential speaking venues you believe to be ideal. You want to be able to tell potential hirers you speak often. Begin to work your network to get speaking spots. Ask friends and clients to introduce you to professional groups they're affiliated with.

Get some training

If you're serious about developing as a speaker, join a Toastmasters club, a Meetup dedicated to speaking, or another relevant association. You might also consider getting some one-on-one training. Speakers often benefit from taking improv or acting classes, which, in addition to being fun, may help you overcome stage fright.

Consider a speakers bureau

You may want to promote your speaking via a speakers bureau. With this approach, you'll pay a fee or percentage of your speaking fees in exchange for gigs.

Package your product

To work with bureaus, you'll need to put together a "speaker's kit." The elements of your speaking kit, listed below, should also be presented on a page of your website.

- A compelling headline
- A brief bio and your photo
- Video of you speaking or a highlight reel
- Topics and session descriptions
- Past speaking gigs
- Testimonials
- Your published works
- Contact form

Also, create a downloadable "one sheet" and/or media kit featuring these elements.

Prepare your speech—and yourself

Mark Twain said, "There are two types of speakers: those that are nervous and those that are liars." The more prepared you are, the better you'll do. Here are some valuable tactics to craft, prepare for, and present your talk:

Create great content
Don't be content to just repeat what you know. Do research, talk to industry leaders, compile the best ideas and stories, and weave them all together with a storyline.

Write it out
While you may improvise well, a good speech is thoroughly planned and includes a strong beginning, middle, and end. The best way to start crafting yours is to write the message you plan to deliver.

Be quotable
Think of sound bites you can offer that beg to be shared via social media: short zingers, impressive stats, or something impactful and memorable. Put your social media handle of

choice and website URL on the slides, so people attribute the quotes to you while they're watching or shortly after.

Make beautiful slides

Plan to use photos, illustrations, screen shots, quotes, graphs, and infographics to deliver an exciting visual element with your speech. Avoid putting too much information on the slides so as to not distract or confuse the audience. Your slides can be impactful even without words.

Practice

The better you know your speech, the better you'll do when it's show time. Practice your speech as much as you can. Ask friends to watch and give you feedback.

Record your practice sessions

If you want to see yourself as the audience will, make videos of your practice sessions. Study your body language. Pay attention to the "ums" and "uhs" you use when thinking aloud. Going too fast? Talking yourself into corners? Pick a few things to improve and try again.

Learn from the pros

There are countless opportunities to see public speakers in action. Watch as many talks as you can, and pay attention to what moves the audience and what puts them to sleep. Think about what you like and don't like. Watching TED Talks online is a great way to start.

Connect early and often

Before, during, and after the event, leverage social media to connect with the organizers, audience, and other speakers. Follow the event online and join the conversation. The point is to build relationships for the long term.

Give a great speech

Your planning is done and now it's time to deliver the goods. Here are some tips to give your best speech ever:

Show up early

Don't stress yourself out by cutting it close. Arrive early and take time to walk the room, meet and greet some of the attendees, and get comfortable with the space.

Test your gear

Things aren't always set up as you expect. Verify your presentation is ready to go. Test the microphone and any equipment you'll use. Walk the stage. Bring a backup copy of your presentation and notes.

Don't read your slides

Avoid "death by PowerPoint." The audience can read much faster than you speak, meaning they're already ahead of you. They don't need you to read the slides to them.

Say no to the lectern

Hiding behind the lectern makes you hard to see. If possible, arrange to stand center stage in full view or to move around a bit.

Be transparent

Speak from truth with uncompromising integrity and authenticity. Don't be afraid to address real issues, problems, and challenges. Don't avoid the tough questions.

Make eye contact

Effective speakers pull their eyes away from their presentation or notes and continuously make eye contact with members of the audience. Doing so will help you concentrate, give you greater confidence, give you feedback, and increase your ability to engage your audience and win their trust. This may take some practice, especially if you're speaking to large groups. You'll want to lock eyes with one person at a time for three to five seconds. You'll often get a little nod of acknowledgement. You can then move gracefully on to someone else in the crowd.

Don't sell

Avoid turning your talk into an ad or product promotion. That's a surefire way not to get invited back. An excellent speech will inspire people to find out more about you and what you have to offer. Make it easy to do so by including a call to action (and possibly an offer) on your final slide. Another great way to conclude your talk is to send the audience home with a challenge. Inspire them to focus on at least one important take-away and forge a plan for taking action.

Stick around

For most events, you should budget time to answer questions from the audience. After you speak, make yourself available to connect with the audience. Take advantage of the built-in conversation icebreaker that speaking in public provides. It's networking nirvana.

Have fun

Do your best to avoid being stiff and formal. Relax and try to be entertaining. Allow yourself to have fun with it.

T

is for

Target

Develop keen insights into your target market

Who cares what you have to say?
Develop a clear understanding of your target market. Develop personas with a focus on the needs of your audience and their pain points. Conduct interviews and surveys to learn as much as possible.

DOUG KESSLER
CO-FOUNDER OF
VELOCITY PARTNERS

Targeting is as much about knowing whom you're NOT aiming for as knowing whom you'll be great for. Some of this will come down to demographics, but it's also about psychographics: understanding the psychology of your target audience, knowing their preferences and prejudices, their self images, their attitudes towards the challenges in their lives and their work.

Persona documents are important, but even more important is spending time with people in your target audience. Buy them coffee. Pick their brains. Listen to the words they use to talk about their lives. This is gold dust to anyone trying to build a personal brand based on serving people. (That's you, right?)

T is for Target

Targeting is tricky. Inexperienced marketers tend to blow it badly. They want to be everything to everyone—a highly flawed strategy. Actually, it's not a strategy at all because satisfying an objective calls for taking aim at it. You have to identify the target.

Some epic marketing campaigns come to mind when I think about targeting. In the 1980s, when Apple introduced "computers for the rest of us," they made it clear the Macintosh was for those who didn't want to read manuals.

"Silly rabbit, Trix are for kids," claimed the breakfast cereal brand.

A modern example I like to reference is Freshbooks, whose accounting software is for small business owners who lack accounting skills but can't afford to outsource the tasks.

Say you're a social media marketing specialist. Which would be the better plea for new business?

- I can help you with your social media.

- I can help you build a loyal following of impassioned millennials on Instagram.

The first angle is obviously broad. The second represents a targeted approach. While it may not apply to everyone, it will have much greater appeal to some. See, it qualifies the prospective audience and specifically defines the value you bring to the table.

Targeting the people and organizations you are uniquely qualified to help is an all-important strategy for your personal brand development. Why?

- You'll gain a firm grip on the content you should develop and channels to pursue.

- You'll create a deeper, more meaningful connection with the people who matter to your career.

- You'll successfully position yourself in the minds of your audience and thereby attract the right constituents.

First, answer the basic questions

Put some thought into defining the "who, what, when, where, why, and how" that apply to your career and your efforts to build recognition as an expert.

- **Who?** Who are your current customers, partners, potential referral sources, and influential friends? Will segmenting help your cause? Who do you compete with?

- **What?** What problems are you most qualified to solve? What questions can you answer?

- **When?** When does the solution you offer matter most?

- **Where?** Where does your audience seek help?

- **Why?** Why are you doing what you do? Why would someone care? Why are your skills and offerings meaningful?

- **How?** H is for help, right? How can you help?

A mission statement—with a compelling benefit—should come from this exercise.

For example: Seth Price and Barry Feldman offer actionable advice to help people build a recognizable personal brand to advance their careers. (That sounds like an excellent idea for a book.)

Dig deeper with personas

Your brand needs two audiences: (1) the sweet spot, the bull's-eye at the center of the target, a member of a clearly defined audience that has needle-moving power, and (2) a secondary set of people with relevant interests and influence.

Focus on the first. Is it a buyer, the boss, publisher, recruiter? Who is it? What makes them tick? The answer should take the form of a "persona," a fictional biography and characterization of a person who is your ideal target. A persona documents the person's characteristics, needs, and motivations. Done well, it captures both demographics and psychographics.

Demographics:

- Gender
- Job
- Responsibilities
- Location
- Income
- Family life
- Hobbies
- Media consumption habits

Psychographics:

- Motivations
- Challenges
- Needs
- Pain points
- Pleasures
- Personality
- Influences

Your persona can have a little more or a little less information. You make the call. No one's grading it. However, you'll definitely thank yourself for bringing a persona to life. In fact, it's helpful to give that person an easily memorable and meaningful name... Paul Publisher, Beth Bookbuyer, Amy Agent, Tim Traveler.

You can imagine this person on the other side of the desk or the other end of the phone. If you can't, you haven't yet succeeded in personifying your target audience member.

Scope the target, hit the target

Ann Handley, CCO of MarketingProfs and best-selling author, encourages marketers to "develop pathological empathy" for their customers. Great advice. Here are some ideas for doing so:

- **Interview them**—There is simply no better way to understand your target market than to talk to the people in it.

- **Conduct surveys**—If you're building an email list, you can take the pulse of your readers by inviting them to take surveys. Encourage participation by making it fast and easy to answer a short series of specific questions. Offering incentives won't hurt.

- **Mine your Google analytics**—You can uncover all kinds of insights about the interests of those who visit your website by digging into your analytics.

- **Check social media analytics**—Facebook, Twitter, LinkedIn, and most of the social sites also provide their users analytical insights into user behavior.

- **Watch the market**—Use tools such as Google Alerts, Mention, and Buzzsumo to monitor what's being published on relevant topics in your niche and how the audience is responding. Keep tabs on your brand and competitors too.

Targeting begins and ends with understanding your audience and what you can offer them. Be sure to create your personal brand with a specific target in mind.

is for

Unique

THE ROAD TO RECOGNITION

Identify your unique value proposition

What makes you special? Every meaningful brand has a unique value proposition. Though you may be one of millions specializing in your field, you need to develop and nurture a one-of-a-kind point of differentiation.

TED RUBIN

AUTHOR OF *HOW TO LOOK PEOPLE IN THE EYE DIGITALLY*

To quote Dr. Seuss, "Be who you are and say what you feel, because those who mind don't matter and those who matter don't mind." My quirky personality thing is fun socks—the louder and crazier, the better. I take pictures of them when I'm traveling and post them. It's something I've become known for over time. It's a fun part of my personal brand that strikes a chord with many of my business relationships, friends, and followers. I post them to all my social channels, have a hashtag hub on Instagram, a Pinterest board, and Tumblr: We Heart Socks. The important thing is to understand that whatever you do in social channels, it should be genuine and a natural fit for who you are. Think of ways you can involve your social audiences in something that's uniquely you—something that will encourage them to want to interact.Passing your audience's "personality test" is often a good way to get a foot in the door that leads to developing that all-important return on relationship.

U is for Unique

It's unlikely your area of expertise is unique. But you are.

There's no other person on the planet who has your genetic code. We're not going to get into biology here, but we will get into transforming your bio into a memorable and unique value proposition (UVP).

We could probably do without the fancy marketing jargon (and abbreviation) because we're looking at a very simple idea. You need a way to describe how you as an individual uniquely create value for customers, employers, coworkers, and stakeholders.

It relies on developing a central message to differentiate yourself. When you've nailed it, you'll have a short personal branding statement (okay, UVP) that serves you well because it's authentic, unique, and memorable. As is the case with all marketing messages, it should make an emotional connection.

Your XYZ factors

I love the XYZ approach I'm about to describe but can't take credit for it. It comes from PWC, a European company that has created a network of people and professional services firms. To teach lessons on personal branding and help support their members, they brought in the expert William Arruda of Reach Personal Branding.

The approach, abbreviated here, works like this:

Define your X-factor

Your personal brand is strong if—and only if—you can be clear about who you are and where your strengths lie. Begin by documenting your top strengths. In what type of roles do you excel? What are your go-to skills? Which skills are you most excited to use daily? Which are most helpful for achieving your career goals?

Validate your X-factor strengths and skills by bouncing them off your friends and associates in your brand community.

Understand your Y-factor

Next, you'll focus on your values, passions, and purpose in order to create a roadmap focused on steering your career in the right direction. This is your Y (or "Why").

- Begin by identifying your most important values. Rank your top five. Define what each means to you.

- Document your passions. What are your favorite activities? What would you do if money were no issue?

- Explore your purpose. What's your vision? What would you most like to achieve?

- Print your top values, passions, and purpose and place them somewhere where you can see them everyday.

Eliminate your Zzz-factor

PWC claims you must investigate ways to be "a keeper, not a sleeper" (hence the Zzz-factor). Reading excerpts from your resume won't cut it.

But now you have your target nailed (T is for Target). You have your X and Y factors documented. Now, how can you transform your UVP into a little story? (This is commonly called an elevator pitch.)

Imagine yours now. Try drafting it.

"I love photography and animals, which has inspired me to shoot pictures for the local animal shelter, study veterinary science, and bring pets and loving families together."

Wow. You could reel that off to me in the shortest of elevator rides and I'll rack my brain trying to think of a way I can help you achieve your goals.

A great elevator pitch is brief. The person you're speaking to is about to arrive on the floor they're being elevated to. Make it easy to understand, as compelling as possible, as unique as possible—and, of course, 100% true.

Now proposition people

In the end, after examining these questions, organizing your answers, and documenting them, your efforts only matter if you use the resulting pitch. You might have opportunities to do so everyday. You can actually make these opportunities happen.

So get this stuff down. Create an elevator speech featuring your unique value proposition. Put it through the test by trying it out with your family, friends, and mentors. Refine it, memorize it, and then be ready to use it.

You don't want to speak "resume." Resumes are boring. Robots read them now (not potential hirers).

Your past experiences may define where you've come from and what you've accomplished, but the people who matter to your career are thinking in terms of the future.

You need to tell a compelling story to engage people. Use a storytelling approach to demonstrate your passions during conversations and in your online profiles. Give them something personal to chew on. Give them something that differentiates you. Infuse your personality into every form of communications you use. Showcase your unique personal brand.

"PERSONAL BRANDING IS THE ART OF BECOMING KNOWLEDGEABLE, LIKABLE AND TRUSTABLE."
—JOHN JANTSCH

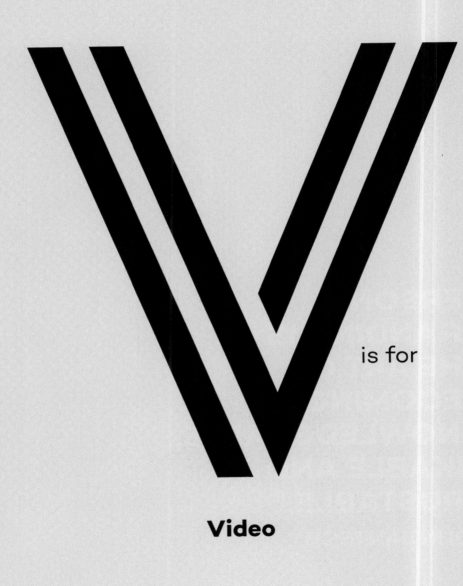

is for

Video

Look into the lens and engage viewers

Roll video into your media mix. Video increases trust and helps you come across as human and sincere. It's become easy to make and distribute video. Look in the lens, relax, and let it roll.

Branding is huge. It can make or break your successes as a professional. And because of this, the time for you to embrace the power of video is now. If you can only afford to do something yourself, then do it. If you can afford to do something professional, even though it might be a financial stretch, make it happen.

MARCUS SHERIDAN

AUTHOR OF *THEY ASK, YOU ANSWER*

FOUNDER OF THE SALES LION

Either way, embrace video. Tell us about you. Tell us your story. What you are is special and it's about time the world understood that a little better, don't you think?

V is for Video

V comes late in the alphabet. It comes late in this book. And it came late in the digital marketing space. It had to.

Our Internet pipes weren't wide enough. Streaming fat video files through skinny connections caused hiccups, interruptions, and all kinds of quality issues contributing to unpleasant experiences with video. We suffered through it a bit while technologists battled the bandwidth issues and pundits prognosticated about a future where video would become omnipresent.

Of course, it's now passé to predict the future of the web is video. According to eMarketer research, in 2015, time spent with digital video surpassed time spent with all other digital platforms. Statistica reports online video reaches more than 90% of U.S. Internet users ages 16 to 44, and more than 80% for older age brackets. You hardly need researchers to get the picture. Simply look around. Video dominates.

Video's not only hot; it's powerful. You can build trust faster with video. More so than text-based communication, video helps people connect with you. You come off as more human and sincere. It allows you to convey your personality, your conviction, and your message. Suffice to say, if you want to build emotional connections with the members of your brand community, it's time to add video to your mix.

Many of your peers aren't yet using video. Most don't have a YouTube channel, a vlog (video blog), or video content of any kind. Making video a part of your personal branding efforts will help you stand out and increase your influence.

Shoot, anyone can do this

Producing video to support your personal branding efforts need not be expensive or difficult. Gone are the days where you had no choice but to hire professionals to script, shoot, narrate, edit, and "air" your video.

Today, your smartphone or computer nearly comprises a full-featured video studio. With the determination to create video, you can be well on your way with a very small budget. The basics will do fine:

- **Camera**—Smartphones, point-and-shoots, or DSLRs all record HD video.

- **Microphone**—Viewers will forgive poor quality video but not sub-par sound. Invest in a decent microphone to assure audio quality.

- **Tripod**—Avoid the shakes by using a tripod unless the camera you're using is stationary.

- **Editing software**—If you want to edit your video after shooting, all you'll need is Movie Maker (Windows) or iMovie (Mac), which are preloaded onto newer computers and devices.

And... action!

Okay, you're ready to roll. What type of videos might you create? The list is long and limited only by your imagination. Here are some ideas you might consider:

- **Bio**—Can't introduce yourself in person? Create a brief video about yourself. A bio video will serve you well on your website and LinkedIn and help you standout.

- **Say hello**—Say hello to a client, partner, employee, or colleague with a friendly and casual video.

- **One-to-one video**—Make videos to follow up on meetings, send a thank-you message, proposal, or anything that you might have otherwise written.

- **Lessons**—Deliver your ideas as you would via a blog post. If you're comfy with the camera, you can simply point and shoot. If you'd rather, you can present images and narrate as you would in a webinar (and as you often see in documentaries). Script (or at least outline) this type of video in advance.

- **Story time**—Tell a little story. Read something you wrote on camera—or anything you believe is worth sharing.

- **Testimonials**—Offer colleagues testimonials via video. Do so unsolicited when you feel strongly about your working relationship with someone. Imagine the impression you'll make.

- **Meetings**—Conduct meetings you can't attend physically via video. Skype, Zoom, Google+ Hangouts, and a heap of affordable web conferencing services make it easy to host highly productive web meetings.

- **Demonstrations**—Show your audience how you do things, what you do, and what you sell.

- **Interviews**—Interview experts for your blog or YouTube channel. You can make a one-on-one video or do a roundup-style video where multiple people contribute. Encourage people to interview you too.

- **Quick thoughts**—Create a series of "thoughts of the day."

- User generated—Ask peers, followers, and friends to make video for you and share it.

- **Social slices**—Simply capture what you're doing and where you are to create fun video segments that unveil little slices of your life.

Video and social media are BFFs

Social media enthusiasts love watching and sharing video. Social media has seen a galactic rise of platforms catering to video and shaping how it's consumed.

- **YouTube**—The granddaddy of online video, YouTube reports 6-billion hours of video are watched each month on its social platform, making it the web's third-most-trafficked site. Nearly 40% of watch-time comes from mobile.

- **Instagram**—Instagram was around for two years before Facebook snagged the company for a cool billion in 2012. Home to both images and short videos, Instagram has been embraced by all types of brands.

- **Snapchat**—Snapchat is a mobile messaging application used to share photos, videos, text, and drawings. Unlike other social apps, messages quickly disappear from the recipient's phone. A "stories" feature allows users to compile photos and videos for all their friends to view for 24 hours.

- **Pinterest**—Pinterest redefined social bookmarking with its free service enabling users to post (a.k.a. "pin") images and video on "pinboards." A social phenom, Pinterest drives more referral traffic than YouTube, LinkedIn, and Google+ combined.

- **Tumblr**—A cross between a social networking site and blog, Tumblr makes it easy to share any type of media.

- **Facebook**—Facebook has made a clear commitment to video, especially with its Facebook Live feature for mobile users. Features are being developed quickly for the app, and it appears live video content is favored in news streams.

- **Twitter**—Like Facebook, Twitter has been developing its video features. Twitter offers a mobile app enabling you to capture, edit, and share video. You can also post video from any device, provided it fits the (frequently changing) length limit.

- **Google+**—While Google+ is a very video-friendly network, its videoconferencing Hangouts feature sets it apart. In addition to its ability to record multiple participants at once, Hangouts make it possible to share screens, files, and presentations, or just chat.

- **LinkedIn**—So far, LinkedIn has stayed away from native video but does allow posting videos on updates or embedding YouTube video on its blog publishing platform.

- **SlideShare**—A LinkedIn company, SlideShare is mostly used as a forum for sharing presentations; however, users can embed YouTube video in their SlideShare presentations.

"Roll" with the changes

Video is a major force in digital marketing now, but it's a rollercoaster ride due, in large part, to the rise in mobile consumption. New strategies, platforms, and features are literally twisting and turning the environment upside-down and sideways. Case in point: some services allow you to shoot and share video in a vertical format.

Live streaming is the wildest part of the ride for social media marketers. It's coming of age and bringing a real-time audience to Facebook, Twitter, YouTube, and additional channels.

Video is also transitioning from passive to interactive, a trend bound to proliferate. Viewers will have more options to choose their own adventure as "watching" transforms to "experiencing."

We've just scratched the surface. Video is the new sweetheart of the always-on media world but is evolving so quickly, it's easy to forget, just a few years ago, there were few options for video in social media.

While this chapter's largely about encouraging you to add video to your media mix, these final words on the topic are to encourage you to stay tuned. Video has arrived, but changes will continue coming fast and furiously. Roll with them.

"PERSONAL BRANDING IS ABOUT BUILDING AUTHORITY THAT GETS PEOPLE TO PAY ATTENTION TO YOUR MESSAGE AND WANT TO SHARE AND RECOMMEND IT TO OTHERS."

—MARK TRAPHAGEN

is for

W

Website

Construct a home on the web in your name

Master your domain. Your website is the mousetrap and your content is the cheese. Work with professionals to plan, design, write, and publish a website that is the HQ of your personal brand.

Social media is great for engagement and reach, but the goal of any brand, especially a personal one, is to build a community around an online property you own. Ownership gives you control and allows you to evolve independent of the tools and social channels used to engage with a community.

FREDERICK TOWNES
CO-FOUNDER OF
PLACESTER

To be successful
in the long term,
you need to
have a digital
destination—a
website—that you
control and leverage
to develop your
brand.

W is for Website

You need a website. It's your home on the web, the hub of the content you create and a destination for each and every member of the network you're building to power your way down *The Road to Recognition*.

"But wait," you might say, "I have a LinkedIn page. I have all kinds of stuff going on in social media channels. Do I really need a website too?" You do.

The content you post on social media networks belongs to those networks. You need to own your brand and purposefully direct it. You do that first and foremost with your website, which allows you to:

- Project yourself the way you want, the way you control.

- Stand out from those you compete with.

- Globalize your reach.

- Create connections with like-minded people.

- Create a calling card that's far more compelling than a business card.

Named site vs. brand... or both?

This chapter is devoted to showing you the way to create a website for your personal brand that's credible, visible, scalable, and user-friendly. It may feel like an intimidating process, but it's manageable if you take it one step at a time.

Establish your domain

Creating a website calls for a number of technical considerations, including securing your domain name, contracting with a web hosting service provider, and selecting a platform that will serve your needs.

- **Domain name**—Your domain name is your address on the web. Investigate your options at a domain name registrar service. If you can't secure a .com (your name.com), buy the rights to use .net, .me, or another suffix that suits you.

- **Web hosting**—Select a company to serve as your website host and then a specific package from their service offerings. You can be frugal when you make the choice and upgrade to a higher performance package in the future when the need arises.

- **Website platforms**—Content management systems (CMS) give you control of your website design, functionality, and performance. Functionality varies from platform to platform, but all CMSs give you the ability to edit and update your website quickly. WordPress is the most popular CMS platform by far, used on over 15 million websites across the web. Because WordPress is so popular, it's easy to find designs, plugins, developers, and services to help you create the website you want.

Website builders such as Squarespace, Wix, and Weebly allow you to create websites using a template and drag-and-drop interface. Website builders are inexpensive and spare you from dealing with coding, software maintenance, or other technical aspects. However, website builders may be too limited to fulfill your needs as they expand.

Make a plan

Unless you're up for learning all the tricks of the trade, you'll work with at least one or two people to create your website. You can make the process smoother and faster with:

- **Website map**—A smart starting point for structuring your website is to create a site map. You can do so with a simple list of pages, a spreadsheet, or basic flow chart.

- **Wireframes**—Wireframing is a popular technique to plan navigation, page layout, and the basic structure of web pages before the actual design work begins. A wireframe is usually done in black and white so the focus is strictly on mapping the page and placing individual elements. Wireframes can be sketched on paper, created with PowerPoint or Keynote, or with online wireframing tools.

- **Creative brief**—A creative brief document helps take your project from concept to completion. It should articulate a set of objectives and summarize the factors that will impact the website's development, such as: objectives, audience, competitors, tone, message, visuals, design preferences, budget, and any other details to help the team get on the same page.

A smart start strategy

Though many platforms make it easy to get started on your website, getting the return on investment you want will likely require bringing in some experts. A complete website production team covers:

- Copywriting
- Graphic design
- Development
- Search engine optimization
- Conversion

Tackle the roles you feel comfortable with and hire experts to help with the rest. When working with your team, especially with designers and developers, I propose a "smart start" strategy, which simply calls for referencing designs you like. Go web surfing in search of websites that feature design ideas and elements that turn you on.

Makes notes regarding the elements you feel are a fit for your website and share them with your team. Mix, match, and make these strategies work to serve your purposes.

Put the pieces in place

Here are many common website elements, which you might want to include.

- **Header**—The header of your website should be elegant and uncluttered, with the logo in the upper left corner. Place the menu in the same position all across your site and ensure it looks and operates consistently.

- **Hero shot**—Your hero shot is the main image on your home page and, along with its headline, should inspire the right visitors to interact further. Avoid corny stock photos. For a personal branding site, a professional photo of you is appropriate.

- **Calls to action**—Each page should have an objective and strive to achieve it with a call to action. Provide simple, clear directions and make sure they're easy to see and easy to follow.

- **Forms**—To collect visitor information, subscription forms and other forms may appear on landing pages, a "contact us" page, in the main body of any page, or in a sidebar or footer. To increase conversion, request only the information you need and no more.

- **Trust builders**—Elements you can feature on your web pages to foster trust include:

  - Testimonials

  - Accolades and awards

  - Certifications

  - Memberships

  - Security symbols

  - Various types of "earned" badges

  - Ratings and reviews

  - Policy statements

  - Guarantees

- **Internal site search**—Offer your visitors a mechanism to search for content on your site.

- **Share buttons**—Add social sharing buttons (often presented in bars) to make it easy for visitors to share your content via their social network accounts.

- **Follow buttons**—Use social media follow buttons to make it easy to connect on your social pages.

- **Web forms**—Place a form on your contact page and other places on your site where it makes sense.

- **Footer**—It's useful to place important information and quick-access links in your website's footer.
- **Additional elements**—Depending on what you do, you may want to include:

  - Membership access
  - A portfolio
  - Links to your blog, content hub, and resources
  - Features and benefits of your product and/or service

Website design considerations

Steve Jobs famously said, "Design is not just what it looks like and feels like. Design is how it works." Your goal is to balance intuitive navigation with engaging design to help visitors quickly find what they seek and deliver a positive customer experience.

- Eliminate clutter and remove anything that isn't necessary.
- Organize content logically, in buckets, so to speak.
- Avoid features such as complex animations, auto-play videos, and music.
- Plan your page top-down, where messages are presented in order of importance.
- Select colors and images that work well in a cohesive design.
- Use white space (or negative space) between graphics, columns, images, text, margins, and other elements. The use of white space creates a feeling of comfort and elegance and guides the eye to important elements.
- Avoid reader fatigue with sizable text, narrow line lengths, and ample leading (the space between lines of copy).
- Make most page layouts uniform across your site to maintain a clean, organized feeling.

Tips for writing your most important pages

Here's a quick set of writing pointers for your most important pages, the pages that have become standards for the majority of websites.

Homepage

Write the homepage copy to function as the lobby of your website. Its main purpose is to direct readers a level deeper into your site—to engage them. Think along the line of, "Hi, stick around and click around."

- Write a big, bold headline that conveys a sense of belonging. The ideal headline should qualify the reader by saying, "You're in the right place if..."

- A clear and concise introduction should follow. Don't get self-serving and boring. Remain focused on the readers' desires.

- Use, but don't overuse, keywords, key phrases, and derivatives of them. Be deliberate for the search engines but natural for the reader.

About page

Your About page is sure to be one of the most visited pages on your website. Don't make it a snoozer.

- Be interesting. You want the reader to want to know more about you, not less. Make every line interesting and support your value proposition.

- Write in a friendly tone, avoiding stiff and boring mission and vision statements that reek of press releases.

- Don't inflate your story. Be wary of superlatives and hyperbole. Establish credibility by being honest.

- Have some fun here. This is your website. Infuse it with your personality. Try video. Quotes. Fun images. Make your About page a page that could only reside on your website.

Landing pages

The following tips speak to pages created to solicit an opt-in or a desired action from a visitor. A landing page is not about helping people find what they want; it's about delivering it.

Make a deliberate keyword connection. Visitors came by way of a search query, a social media post, an ad, or an email. It's important that they feel they've landing on the right page after clicking through. Connect the dots by clearly restating in your headline the keywords that drove them here.

- Focus solely on the offer. Stay on point and do not offer any links or elements that could potentially reduce conversion.

- Hammer home the value being offered with action words. Answer the questions, "why this" and "why now," in no uncertain terms.

- Show your offer and describe it in a caption. In fact, it's a good idea to make every section of your landing page have some stand-alone power that reiterates the promise.

- Make your form short and simple. The more information you require, the fewer opt-ins you'll generate.

- Use social proof, especially testimonials.

- Make your buttons work. Avoid generic "asks." Try short, directive value statements such as "Send me my free tips."

Contact pages

You don't want to overlook the page prospects head to when they want to get in touch.

- As with a landing page, fewer fields equals more responses.

- Increase responses by increasing contact options. In addition to a form, consider offering email (and/or specific email addresses), phone, fax, text, chat, and even a mailing address.

- There's no reason your contact page shouldn't be a fun part of the website, reflect your brand, and add to the customer experience.

Optimize each page

SEO is a topic for another book (See SEO Simplified for Short Attention Spans, by Barry). However, with optimized pages, you generate more traffic, leads, and sales through your website, so we'll scratch its surface with some basics here.

If you're new to SEO, I want you to know it's not as frightening or complex as you might imagine, nor is it difficult to understand the essential elements of optimizing your site for search.

The foundation of your SEO relies on effectively implementing basic optimization across your website. It begins with keyword research. Your challenge is to identify the words your target audience uses to search for content.

Be forewarned: with a new website, you won't do well to select broad, highly competitive keywords. Instead, follow the tips below to select "long-tail" keywords with less competition.

Try brainstorming to get started. Evaluate the topics your website focuses on and create a list. Graduate next to expanding your list of keyword ideas with keyword discovery tools, including the free Google AdWords Keyword Tool. Check out the keywords your competitors use with SEMrush or Alexa by Amazon.

Finally, cull your keyword ideas into a shortlist of the most promising keywords and phrases for your website. To accomplish this, equip yourself with data insights from Open Site Explorer and the MozBar tool, both from Moz. Your challenge in this phase is to estimate the difficulty for ranking for each keyword. Ideally, you need to aim for keywords where the competition is modest and the websites that rank for them are comparable to yours in terms of authority.

When you're ready to place the keywords you've chosen on your pages, be careful not to overdo it. Search engines will penalize keyword-stuffed pages. Keep it simple by using one to five keyword phrases per page and optimize each with natural language.

How to optimize your pages

According to Moz, an ideally optimized web page is hyper-relevant to a specific topic. How do you achieve hyper-relevance? First and foremost, the page must provide unique and useful content on the subject. Additionally, the page must be "marked up" in its code so keywords are:

- Included in the title tag.
- Included in the URL.
- Used within the copy of the page.
- Included in the alt text of the images on-page.

Fear not. Coding skills are not necessary. When you get comfortable with your CMS, you'll find marking up or "tagging" page elements is easily done within the editor or an SEO plugin such as Yoast SEO.

Write compelling meta descriptions. The irony here is thick. Meta description is a very unfriendly term for a little optimization exercise you'll do to make each page appear user friendly.

Meta descriptions do not actually help with page rankings. Written well, they help earn clicks (which actually will affect how the page ranks). See, a meta description suggests to search engines how the snippet of copy that appears in your search engine results page (SERP) listing should read.

Write meta descriptions that:

- Explain the page's content to searchers.
- Employ your keywords intelligently—they'll be bolded if they match the search.
- Adhere to the space limitations (which are subject to change). Longer snippets will be cut off with an ellipsis (...).

Is that all there is to it?

On-page and off, there's always more to search engine optimization than you (or anyone) could know. Search algorithms change relentlessly. They're kept secret. And the powers that be will never totally reveal the secrets.

The best you can do is gather insights from experts who analyze SEO, experiment with the practices they propose, and control what you can.

For further on-site search optimization:

- **Create internal links**—Help search engines learn more about your website by internally linking to other pages within your content.

- **Use header tags**—Various levels of HTML header tags (H2 and H3, for example) help break your content into sections and tell search engines what each section is about.

- **Deliver a speedy and reliable website**—Slow-loading web pages and website uptime issues negatively affect rankings.

- **Create a responsive site**—Mobile-friendly websites are rewarded with higher rankings on mobile searches and labeled "mobile friendly."

is for

eXamine

Keep close tabs on your progress

Measure what matters. Your x-ray for all online efforts is analytics. Deploy Google Analytics and/or additional tools to stay informed of how visitors behave on your site and what you can do to improve their experience.

ANDY CRESTODINA

AUTHOR OF *CONTENT CHEMISTRY*

CO-FOUNDER OF ORBIT MEDIA STUDIOS

Want to be known for something? You have to publish on that topic—a lot. And whether or not your 50th article, podcast, or video gets a lot of traction—or just a little—has to do with whether you've paid attention to the results of the first 49. If you watch your website, social media, and email marketing analytics, you're going to get a little smarter, reach a little farther, and grow awareness of your brand more quickly. Otherwise, you're flying blind.

I read an interview of Will Smith once. Way back in the 90s, he decided that he wanted to make one of the top grossing films of all time, so he looked at the list of the top ten. He noticed it was filled with sci-fi special effects movies. So he decided to make Men In Black, which became one of the top 10 grossing films of all time. That's a simple example of how data can be used to make smart decisions.

X is for eXamine

I just did a search for "personal branding + analytics." I got 180 results. A few offered insights regarding analytics tools. Most didn't offer any useful information. I think it's fair to say this chapter will be the only thing you've ever read on the subject of personal branding measurement. Hmph.

As you've probably read before, you can't manage what you don't measure. (I got 32.9 million results on that search.) It's a fact of life—and business—but still, sometimes it's an eye-opener.

Get insights and get better

By now, as you get into the 24th chapter of the book, you've gathered that the content you create and publish is immensely meaningful to your brand. Ten of the chapters dug into things you can—and should—examine regularly in an effort to measure your progress.

- Blog
- Content
- Email
- Followers (social media)
- Google
- LinkedIn
- Offers
- Podcast
- Video
- Website

If you want each of the above to perform for you, you need to track them. You don't need to be a statistics pro or analytics mastermind. You simply need to learn how you're doing, so you can perpetually refine your efforts.

Basic analytics is easy

In any type of marketing, brands that embrace and effectively use analytics will be more successful than those that don't. Data analysis provides insights into your audience: their preferences and desires. It offers you insights into the efficacy of your strategy and personal branding tactics and provides actionable information on which you can base important decisions.

Are you averse to number crunching? Fear not. Digital media makes it simple to track your efforts through the use of data and analytics so you can make informed decisions to increase your impact. The key is not to let the data overwhelm you. Let it be your guide.

Google Analytics comes first

Google Analytics is your staple. The most used platform for data collection on web properties, it offers a host of tools that can help you gather important insights. The tool is free and easy to put in place with a line of code.

As a starting point, use Google Analytics to examine:

- **Page views**—Learn which pages are attracting visitors.
- **Referring sites**—Determine where your traffic comes from.
- **Engagement**—Look at time on page, pages per session, and session duration to assess engagement.
- **Demographics**—Information about age, gender, interests, geography, and more is available at a glance.

Examine what matters

We covered a good deal of analytics that are meaningful for your blog and website, but where there's digital marketing, there's data, which you can mine to your heart's content.

- **Every kind of content**—Every content channel you contribute to offers useful metrics—whether it be for video (YouTube), slide decks (SlideShare), public blog communities (Medium), infographics, podcasts, etc.

- **Email**—Your email service provider delivers reporting that enables you to gauge open rates, click-through rates, unsubscribes, and more.

- **Search**—A variety of tools, free and paid, will help track the progress you're making with search.

- **Social media**—Every social platform provides meaningful metrics.

- **Conversion**—You can track the results you're getting from offers and the various forms on your website and blog, either with Google Analytics (setup required) or landing page and marketing automation subscription services.

The metrics market is huge

At last count, there were roughly one-zillion digital marketing tools available. Though most can be useful for the personal brander, you may have noticed we've been reluctant to endorse them in this book. It's not for political or financial reasons. It's because they come and go fast.

So throwing caution to the wind now, here's a shortlist of some favorites you should consider using (circa 2017 and, hopefully, beyond):

- **Media monitoring**—Set up Google Alerts to deliver timely mentions of your name, company, products, or any topic to your inbox. Mention (free and paid versions) is also a strong media tracking tool.

- **Social shares**—Buzzsumo, another free and paid tool, rules for tracking social media shares by website, topic, or author. It recently added a column that reports the number of backlinks the content has earned.

- **More social metrics**—Simply Measured delivers many types of social analytics. Buffer is a remarkable tool for scheduling social shares as well as gathering performance data.

- **Influence**—Though it's much maligned, Klout is a simple service you can use to keep tabs on your social influence (and more). Kred is another.

Make a KPI dashboard and make your move

Again, don't allow the maze of metrics and analytics tools to make your head spin. Keep it simple as you get started. Consider creating a dashboard or scorecard in the form of a spreadsheet or table to track the metrics you feel are most meaningful for the development of your personal brand.

You might set it up with just a handful of metrics—say, for example, website traffic, Twitter followers, social shares, and email list growth. Record these numbers (or any numbers you want) monthly. Whether you do or don't like the numbers, you'll gather important insights simply by examining them.

Keep in mind, you don't do analytics only to create reports. Do it to inform your decisions. Ask yourself questions. Find the answers in the numbers and take action based on them.

is for the **"You Do" List**

Make a plan to achieve your personal branding goals

Know what you're doing? The development of your personal brand is a perpetual exercise. Create a plan for getting started as well as a list of proactive actions YOU DO regularly.

NAVID MOAZZEZ
LIFESTYLE ENTREPRENEUR
AND FOUNDER OF VIRTUAL
SUMMIT MASTERY

Building a profitable personal brand online is not a sprint or something that happens overnight. Don't aim for perfection early on.

Instead, allow your brand to evolve naturally over time and focus on providing massive value and over-deliver to your target audience.

Then your message and brand will get clearer.

Y is for the "You Do" List

Get a list together. Things you need to do long term. Things you'll do in the quarter to come. Things you'll do on an ongoing basis. Here are action items to put on your "You Do" list or lists. Come up with a system for creating and referencing them.

A is for Authenticity

- Define your area of expertise as specifically as possible.
- Create a list of your attributes, skills, and strengths. Hit up friends for input. How do they describe you?
- Create a list of your values.

B is for Blog

- Define your blogging objectives.
- Document a mission statement for your blog.
- Develop an editorial plan and idea file.
- Monitor your market continuously.
- xperiment with different types of posts to establish an interesting mix.
- Practice your writing to perpetually improve.
- Publish regularly.

C is for Content

- Research the needs and behaviors of your target market.
- Identify leaders in your niche, take inventory of their content, and consume as much as you can.
- Create a list of the content formats you're most likely to use and identify how your strengths align with them.
- Identify keywords you want to use in your content.
- Conceive an idea for something substantial—a piece of "big content"—and make a plan for how you'll repurpose the work.

- Create a list of media channels and tactics you'll rely on to promote your content.

D is for Design

- Develop a logo, color palette, and design standards.

- Get a professional-quality portrait.

- Design and print business cards.

- Determine if you'll have additional design and print needs for collateral, stationery, or your website.

- Create social media profiles that reflect well, and consistently, on your brand.

- Make sure your website and blog conform to your brand design standards.

E is for Email

- Research and select your email service provider.

- Learn how to send different types of email using pre-formatted templates and the tools provided.

- Set up and experiment with techniques to collect email addresses on your website.

- Consider developing segmented lists as needed.

- Plan and write an autoresponder series for new subscribers.

- Explore your options for email types and plan accordingly to automate repetitive tasks and maintain contact with subscribers.

F is for Followers

- Select one or two social media channels to focus your social media efforts, based on your target audience's activity levels.

- Create profile pages using relevant keywords to define your brand.

- Follow like-minded people and influencers in your niche.

- Share relevant content and contribute thoughtful commentary.
- Develop the habit of conducting social media activity daily.

G is for Google

- Google yourself. (Change your setting to "hide private results.")
- Set up Google Alerts for your name and any brands you want to monitor.
- Apply the ideas in this book to steadily improve your personal brand's ability to rank in search.

H is for Helping

- Identify ways to offer your time for consultations, mentorships, community service, etc.
- Create a list of ways you can share helpful content.
- Look at how you might use your resources to create opportunities for others.
- Act as a networking catalyst by connecting people you know with each other.

I is for Influencers

- Use social channels to identify a list of influential people in your niche, focusing on leading content creators.
- Track their work consistently.
- Join the conversations they inspire.
- Find opportunities to create content in collaboration with influencers.
- Recognize and thank your influencers whenever appropriate.

J is for Joining

- Surround yourself with people who are positive influences and challenge you to accomplish more.

- Identify groups worth joining, including trade associations, professional clubs, mastermind groups, networking groups, and community service clubs.
- Join social media groups.
- Pursue networking opportunities with other group members.

K is for Keywords

- Create a short list of keyword phrases you want your brand to be associated with.
- Get familiar with Google AdWords and keyword suggestion tools.
- Work your keywords into your social media profiles.
- Work your keywords into your website and content.

L is for LinkedIn

- Take extreme care to make your LinkedIn profile excellent in every way.
- Build relationships on LinkedIn.
- Deliver valuable content on LinkedIn.

M is for Media

- Analyze the media footprint of your competition and industry influencers.
- Ask your audience questions regarding their media preferences.
- Repurpose your content across different media to increase your reach.
- Link off-site assets back to your website and blog.
- Work toward ensuring brand continuity across your media assets.

N is for Network

- Create and refine basic networking tools such as your business card, resume, and social media profiles.

- Meet people and establish beneficial relationships.

O is for Offers

- Choose a magnetic topic and create a free offer based on it. Repeat.
- Try a variety of content formats and lead magnet styles.
- Showcase your offer wherever you publish content to continuously build your email list.

P is for Podcast

- Strive to get interviewed on existing podcasts.
- Create your own podcast program.
- Promote your podcast or programs you were a guest on.

Q is for Questions

- Pose questions to yourself regarding your personal brand for self-reflection and goal setting.
- Sharpen your listening skills by using questions.
- Listen for questions online and try to answer them.

R is for Recognizing Others

- Collaborate on a project with someone who inspires you.
- Recognize someone via social media or on your blog.
- Contribute to a blog.
- Connect associates to each other.
- Deliver a sincere "thank you."

S is for Speaking

- You can do it. Say it: "I'm a speaker."
- Get some speaker training.
- Create a speaker's kit.
- Promote yourself as a speaker and apply for speaking opportunities.
- Prepare, practice, and present.

T is for Target

- Determine how to appeal to a highly specific audience.
- Create audience personas.
- Develop empathy by getting to know their needs.

U is for Unique

- Define your X-factor by documenting your strengths.
- Define your "Why" factor by documenting your passions and purpose.
- Practice, improve, and perfect your elevator pitch by trying it out on people.

V is for Video

- Get some basic video equipment.
- Review the various types of videos and do some planning.
- Shoot and publish.

W is for Website

- Secure a domain, web host, and CMS.
- Plan your website, the components of your website, and determine your resource needs.
- Write great website copy or hire a copywriter to help.
- Optimize each page for search.
- Test your site's performance.

X is for eXamine

- Set up Google Analytics on your website.
- Check it often.
- Identify additional analytics tools you'll use to monitor your progress with content, email, search, social media, and conversion.
- Identify the metrics that matter most for the growth of your personal brand.

Y is for your "You Do" List

- Decide on an effective way to create, review, and update your You Do list.

- Make a list of things you'll do in the near term as a result of reading this book.

- Make additional lists that suit your working style (daily, weekly, monthly, quarterly, annually) and use them to guide your personal branding pursuits.

Z is for Zeal

- Decide what you want to happen (your objective).

- Make it happen.

"IF YOU DON'T SHARE YOUR IDEAS, NO ONE WILL KNOW IF THEY'RE ANY GOOD."
—DORIE CLARK

is for

Zeal

Let no roadblock slow you down

Shift into overdrive. Zeal is a "strong feeling of interest and enthusiasm that makes one determined to do something." There is no more essential ingredient of a successful personal brand.

ROBERT ROSE

CO-AUTHOR OF
*EXPERIENCES: THE SEVENTH
ERA OF MARKETING*

CHIEF STRATEGY OFFICER
OF CONTENT MARKETING
ADVISORY

Do you feel sometimes you are just going through the motions?

As you drive to work today, run on the treadmill, or wherever the next moment of self-reflection finds you, take a true time out. Focus

on: "What makes
me passionate?"
And every day going
forward, incorporate
small changes to
pursue your answer.
Passion is the only way
you master what you
think you might want
to do.

Give yourself the
gift of passionate
imagination. Find your
zeal. It's what you're
looking for and how
you'll accomplish your
goals.

Ten things that require zero talent:

1. Being on time

2. Work ethic

3. Effort

4. Body language

5. Energy

6. Attitude

7. Passion

8. Being coachable

9. Doing extra

10. Being prepared

Z is for Zeal

You're not going to achieve massive recognition quickly. It takes time and perseverance. You'll encounter obstacles. Some of your ideas may get rejected. People will turn you down. You'll make mistakes and get distracted. Pursuing your dream is hard work.

But you're reading the final chapter of a book about accelerating the development your personal brand. You have what it takes to build a successful personal brand. You don't need to be a genius, a great writer, a gifted videographer, or great speaker.

What you need is zeal. Call it want you like: passion, fervor, enthusiasm, dedication, grit, or commitment. But call on it often because it's what you need most to achieve personal branding success.

"Nearly all rich and powerful people are not notably talented, educated, charming, or good-looking. They became rich and powerful by wanting to be rich and powerful," writes Paul Arden in his great book, *It's Not How Good You Are, It's How Good You Want To Be*. "Your vision of where or who you want to be is the greatest asset you have."

I'm not suggesting your goals need to revolve around money and power. That's for you to decide. My job is to help you establish a powerful personal brand and accelerate your professional success. Your job is to apply yourself in all the ways necessary to achieve your goals.

Zeal is not a personality trait. It's a choice to persist, dig deep, and take action when it feels like things aren't going your way. It's the willingness to overcome exhaustion, resistance, and unfortunate circumstances. It's the courage to work hard and press on.

Re-write your story

Where you currently are in your career is based on decisions you made along the way. Maybe you have a habit of being late. You're not good at public speaking. Or you believe you don't have the time to pursue your dreams. These aren't inherent character traits. These are things you have decided.

It's often easier to accept things about ourselves as truths rather than choices. For example, I remember deciding I couldn't draw. I was ten years old and didn't take into account I was comparing my budding drawing skills to my art professor father who had been practicing for 35 years. From that point on, I ignored all of my art class instructors and didn't practice.

Is there a story you'd like to rewrite about yourself? It's your story. No one can stop you from authoring it the way you'd like.

Work at it
While this book is filled with tactics and strategies to accelerate your professional success, you have to put in the work. Once you decide you want to own your brand, you need to ask yourself, "How hard am I willing to work?"

Quiet the negative voice in your head
The voice in your head may want you to play it safe and stick to your comfort zone. It's the voice that says, "This won't work. I can't do it. I'm not worthy." Talk back to the voice. Prove it wrong.

Take action
If you want to be a writer, write. If you want to be a leader, lead. If you want to be a teacher, teach. There's nothing stopping you but you. Action begets action, just as gym-going begets gym-going and saving begets saving. The hardest part of any good habit is starting. It gets easier with time.

Maintain enthusiasm
Keep your spirits high. Stay focused on your "why." Why do you want what you want? Do you want to be the leader in your field? Do you want to increase your income? Create visual reminders of your "why." Place them where you'll see them every day. Let your future inspire you.

Think outside the box
It's okay to model yourself after your heroes, but don't copy them. Zig when the crowd zags. Take some risks. Push yourself beyond your comfort zone. Travel to see things you

haven't seen before. Study industries other than your own. Sometimes you find the best ideas in unexpected places.

Own it like a boss

You are the CEO and chief bottle washer of your brand. Rid your vocabulary of blame, excuses, whining, and complaining. Be willing to do whatever it takes to achieve your goals.

Go the extra mile

"There are no traffic jams along the extra mile," said NFL Hall of Famer Roger Staubach.

Don't give up. If you stumble, pick yourself up and persevere. Let your zeal drive you further down the road to recognition and to greater professional success.

Acknowledgements

We feel we've created one of the most practical, useful, and actionable resources on personal branding available anywhere. And though we poured ourselves into the project for two years, we hardly traveled down *The Road* alone. The book was fueled by many to whom we are grateful.

Thank you...

Jay Baer, for contributing a leafy, funny, heartfelt foreword, and for your support.

Jan Moscowitz of Studio laPlancha, not only for the wicked design skills that gives this book its unique visual identity but for enduring the Feldman fussiness and Price perfectionism. The road was windy, no doubt, but we are ecstatic about where we arrived.

Kathryn Aragon, for editing the manuscript.

Jeff Maksym, for hauling gads of gear to San Francisco to deliver video and photography used in the book and its promotion.

Everyone who contributed the original content we quoted at the beginning of the chapters, including Kim Garst, Brian Clark, Joe Pulizzi, Richard Moross, Joanna Wiebe, Jeff Bullas, Sujan Patel, Scott Stratten, Lee Odden, Vanessa DiMaura, Brian Dean, Stephanie Sammons, Jason Miller, Scott Abel, Chris Smith, John Lee Dumas, Ian Altman, Bryan Kramer, Michael Port, Doug Kessler, Ted Rubin, Marcus Sheridan, Frederick Townes, Andy Crestodina, Navid Moazzez, and Robert Rose.

Everyone whose ideas were republished, cited, or paraphrased.

Personal brand gurus whose work we've admired and have been inspired by, including William Arruda, Dan Schawbel, Dorie Clark, and Karen Kang.

Our many friends and associates who took time to read advances from the book and deliver reviews and testimonials.

Ann Handley, for arranging the marriage of budding branders Barry Feldman and Seth Price a few years ago, giving birth to our prolific partnership.

The management and team at Placester, for an indescribable heap of support in the making and marketing of the book.

You, for riding this road with us.

With gratitude,

Seth and Barry

About the Authors

Barry Feldman

Digital marketing super freak

After an eight-year stint in the advertising agency business, Barry founded Feldman Creative. LinkedIn, Inc., and many other entities have recognized Barry as a top content marketing and social media influencer and leader.

Over the past 25-plus years, Barry has written marketing copy and provided digital marketing strategy for thousands of companies and entrepreneurs. Barry now specializes in planning and developing content marketing for companies that deliver marketing technology, digital marketing agencies, and software providers.

Barry's writing has touched millions. He's a popular guest blogger published by more than 30 marketing publications, a columnist, and SlideShare keynote author. In 2015, Barry published his first book, SEO Simplified for Short Attention Spans.

Barry is the co-host of the Content Matters podcast, a speaker at marketing conferences, and digital marketing trainer for enterprises and online education specialists.

Barry lives in Folsom, California. He's a husband, father, dog lover, tennis player, musician, and rock and roll maniac.

Connect with Barry
Email: Barry@FeldmanCreative.com
LinkedIn: LinkedIn.com/in/FeldmanCreative

Seth Price

Marketer, motivator, and media maker— executive and entrepreneur

Having consulted for more than 300 companies the past 20 years, Seth is recognized as a business builder and digital marketing specialist. He's passionate about delivering lessons to help business people use media and technology to develop more relevant brands and more rewarding careers.

Seth's currently the Chief Instigator at Placester, home of the Real Estate Marketing Academy, a top educational resource for real estate professionals visited by more than 100,000 marketers each month. Placester is the fourth multimillion-dollar company Seth has helped grow from scratch. As the #3 hire at Placester, Seth has worn all of the go-to-market hats and helped the company build a 450,000-plus customer base in less than five years.

Seth is relentless on the entrepreneurial front as well. He's an in-demand speaker booked over 25 times each year to deliver actionable sessions on personal branding, marketing strategy, and thought leadership. His interview-based programs, Craft of Marketing and Marketing Genius are widely heralded as top marketing strategy podcasts. Seth's a popular guest blogger for numerous publications and advisor to early-stage technology and social media companies, via Startup Institute and Betaspring.

Seth lives in Providence, Rhode Island. He's a husband, father, chef, gardener, and martial arts junkie.

Connect with Seth
Email: Mail@SethPrice.net
LinkedIn: LinkedIn.com/in/SethKPrice

The Road Goes On... Online

Website

Please visit our website: www.theroadtorecognition.com

Mailing list

As our gift to you, our readers and community, the site offers a variety of bonus content available free. Be sure to join our mailing list to get occasional updates about news related to the book.

Community

Join our Facebook group, The Road to Recognition Room, for ongoing discussions and idea exchanges about personal branding.

Support the book

If you liked the book and the content, please tell your friends and share it on your online channels. Also, we'd be grateful if you'd write a review of the book on Amazon or wherever you purchased it. Reviews mean a lot to the authors and the success of the book.

Thank you,
Seth and Barry

Hire the Authors

Seth and Barry are experienced at speaking, training, and coaching on the topic of personal branding, the topics addressed in this book, and more. Consider contacting either or both to:

- Lead a workshop with your organization
- Speak at your meeting or conference
- Deliver personal branding consulting

Media Inquiries

Seth and Barry welcome requests for interviews and are open to inquiries of all types. Resources available at the media page include photos of the book, photos of the authors, and social media content available for sharing.

Please visit:
www.theroadtorecognition.com/media

Notes

Authors cited

Chapter C
Ann Handley, *Everybody Writes: Your Go-To Guide to Creating Ridiculously Good Content* (Wiley, 2014)

Chapter J
Janine Popick, *5 Types of People to Surround Yourself With for Success* (Inc.com, 2015), http://www.inc.com/janine-popick/5-types-of-people-to-surround-yourself-with-for-success.html

Chapter K
Dan Schawbel, *Quotes*, http://danschawbel.com/quotes/

Glen Llopis, *3 Ways To Most Effectively Communicate Your Personal Brand* (Forbes.com, 2013) http://www.forbes.com/sites/glennllopis/2013/07/15/3-ways-to-most-effectively-communicate-your-personal-brand/#1fd590fbefbe

Chapter P
Jerod Morris, *The Single Most Important Reason Why You Should Start a Podcast* (Copyblogger, 2015) http://www.copyblogger.com/why-start-podcast/

Chapter Q
"SCAMPER: Improving Products and Services," (Mindtools) https://www.mindtools.com/pages/article/newCT_02.htm

Chapter R
Michael Stelzner, *Launch: How to Quickly Propel Your Business Beyond the Competition* (Wiley, 2011)

Andy Crestodina, *15 Ways to Say Thank You to Your Network* (Orbit Media, 2016) https://www.orbitmedia.com/blog/ways-to-say-thank-you/

Chapter S

Lee W. Frederiksen, Elizabeth Harr, and Sylvia S. Montgomery, *The Visible Expert* (Hinge, 2014)

Chapter U

"Stand Out Online," (PWC, 2017) http://www.pwc.com/us/en/careers/campus/programs-events/personal-brand/stand-out-online.html

"US Adults Spend 5.5 Hours with Video Content Each Day" (eMarketer, 2015) https://www.emarketer.com/Article/US-Adults-Spend-55-Hours-with-Video-Content-Each-Day/1012362#sthash.nalxYYRX.dpuf

Chapter Z

Paul Arden, *It's Not How Good You Are, It's How Good You Want To Be* (Phaidon Press, 2003)

Brands cited

99 Designs, https://99designs.com/

Adobe Audition, http://www.adobe.com/products/audition.html

Alexa, http://www.alexa.com

Amazon, https://www.amazon.com/

Answers.com, http://www.answers.com/

Audacity, http://www.audacityteam.org/

Buffer, https://buffer.com/

Business Network International, https://www.bni.com

Buzzsumo, https://buffer.com/

Camtasia, https://www.techsmith.com/camtasia.html

Fiverr, https://www.fiverr.com/

FreshBooks, https://www.freshbooks.com/

Garage Band, http://www.apple.com/mac/garageband/

Google AdWords, https://adwords.google.com/home/

Google AdWords Keyword Planner, https://adwords.google.com/home/tools/keyword-planner/

Google Alerts, https://www.google.com/alerts

iMovie, http://www.apple.com/imovie/

iTunes, http://www.apple.com/itunes/

Kathryn Aragon, https://kathrynaragon.com/

Keywordtool.io, http://keywordtool.io/

Klout, https://klout.com/home

Kred, http://www.go.kred/

Libsyn, https://www.libsyn.com/

Meetup, https://www.meetup.com/

Mention, https://mention.com/

Movie Maker, https://www.microsoft.com/en-us/store/p/movie-maker-free-video-editor/9nblggh4wwjr

Moz, https://moz.com/

Placester, http://placester.com/

Quora, https://www.quora.com/

SEMRush, https://www.semrush.com/

Simply Measured, http://simplymeasured.com/

Skype, https://www.skype.com/

SoundCloud, https://soundcloud.com/

Squarespace, https://www.squarespace.com/

StackExchange, http://stackexchange.com/

Statistica, https://www.statista.com/

Stitcher, https://www.stitcher.com/

Studio laPlancha, http://www.laplancha.co/

TED Talks, https://www.ted.com/talks

Toastmasters, https://www.toastmasters.org/

Übersuggest, https://ubersuggest.io/

Udemy, https://www.udemy.com/

Upwork, https://www.upwork.com/

Weebly, https://www.weebly.com/

Wix, http://www.wix.com/

WordPress, https://wordpress.org/

Yahoo! Answers, https://answers.yahoo.com/

Yoast SEO, https://yoast.com/wordpress/plugins/seo/

Zoom.us, https://zoom.us/

Index